BAHRAIN

Gulf Heritage in Transition

Michael Jenner

Longman

London and New York

Longman Group Limited,
Longman House, Burnt Mill, Harlow,
Essex, CM20 2JE, England
and Associated Companies throughout the world

First published 1984
ISBN 0 582 78379 8

British Library Cataloguing in Publication Data

Jenner, Michael
    Bahrain, Gulf heritage in transition.

    1. Bahrain — History.   2. Bahrain — Description
and travel — Views.   I. Title.
DS247.B25J46   1984   953'.65   84-5704
ISBN 0-582-78379-8

Library of Congress Cataloging in Publication Data

Jenner, Michael
    Bahrain.
    1. Bahrain — History
    I. Title
    953'.65   DS247.B25

Set in 10/13pt Monophoto Photina

Printed and bound by Arnoldo Mondadori, Verona,
Italy

CONTENTS

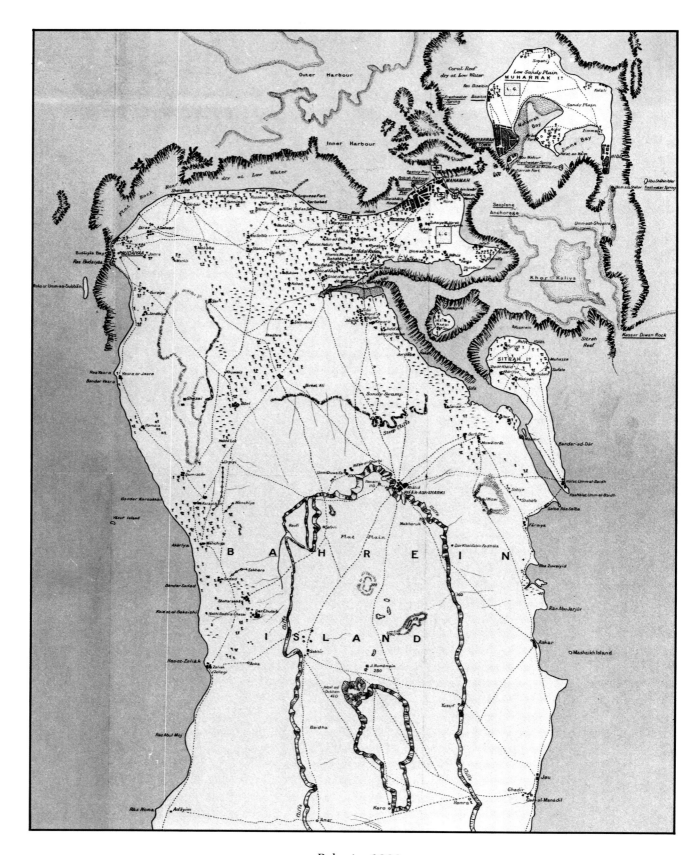

Bahrain, 1933

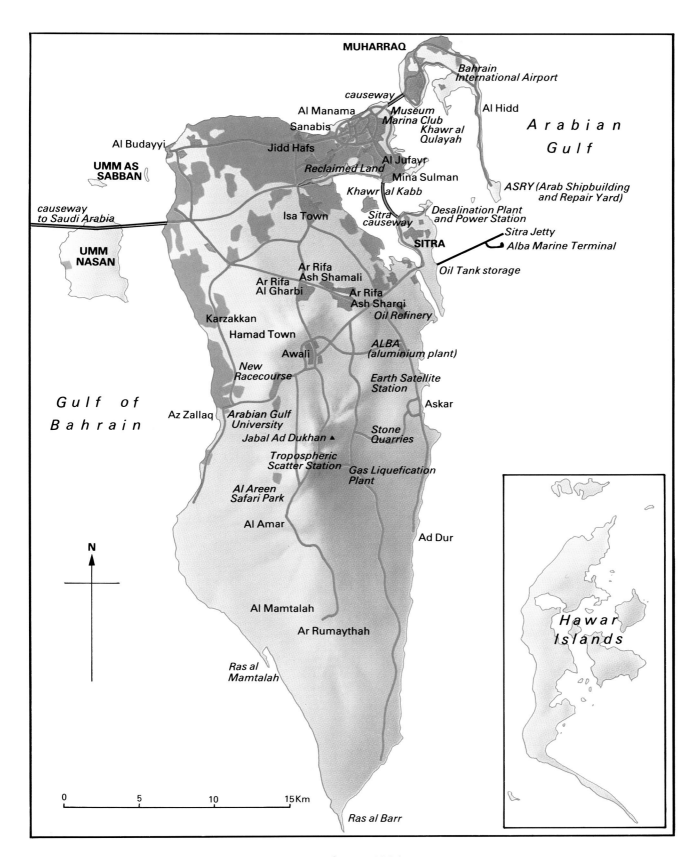

MUHARRAQ

Bahrain
International Airport

causeway

Al Manama   Museum   Al Hidd
Sanabis   Marina Club
                  Khawr al
                  Qulayah   *A r a b i a n*
Al Budayyi   Jidd Hafs   *G u l f*

UMM AS
SABBAN   Al Jufayr
          Reclaimed Land   Mina Sulman
causeway   ASRY (Arab Shipbuilding
to Saudi Arabia   *Khawr al Kabb*   and Repair Yard)
                                      Desalination Plant
UMM   *Sitra*   and Power Station
NASAN   Isa Town *causeway*
                                              Sitra Jetty
                              SITRA   Alba Marine Terminal

                  Ar Rifa   Oil Tank storage
                  Ash Shamali
          Ar Rifa
          Al Gharbi   Ar Rifa
                           Ash Sharqi
Karzakkan   *Oil Refinery*
          Hamad Town
                           ALBA
          Awali   *(aluminium plant)*

Gulf of *New*   *Earth Satellite*
Bahrain *Racecourse*   *Station*
                                      Askar
          Az Zallaq *Arabian Gulf*
                     University   *Stone*
                  Jabal Ad Dukhan ▲ *Quarries*

N   *Tropospheric*
                   Scatter Station *Gas Liquefication*
                                      Plant
          Al Areen
          Safari Park

          Al Amar
                                      Ad Dur

          Al Mamtalah

          Ar Rumaythah   *H a w a r*
                                   I s l a n d s
      Ras al
      Mamtalah

0   5   10   15 Km

                                   Ras al Barr

Bahrain, 1984

Café. Manamah

Traditional dhow building

New central market. Muharraq

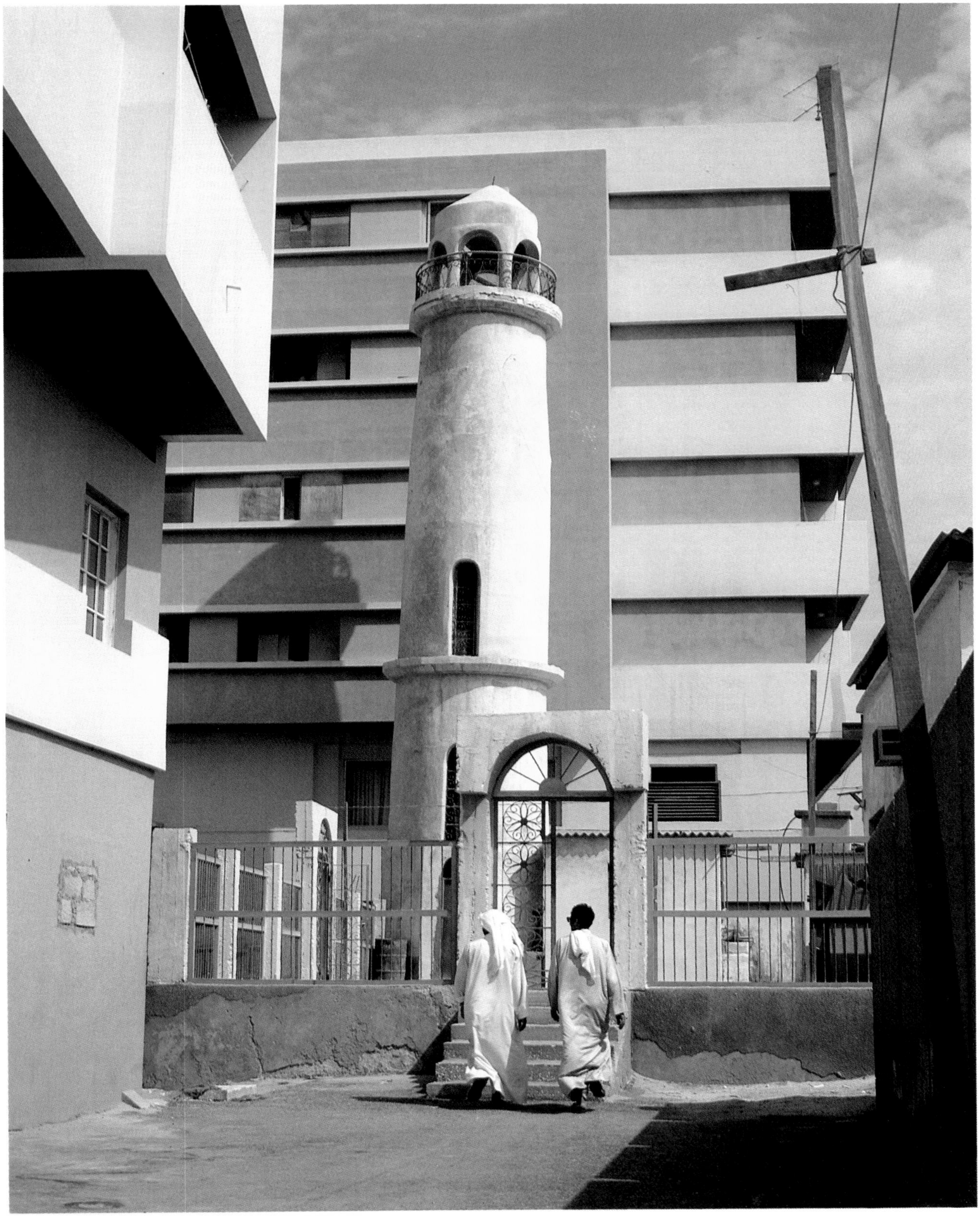

Old and new. Manamah

Traditional interior

Traditional hospitality

A Mosque on Bahrein. From a rough sketch by DE A. Mackell.

ACKNOWLEDGEMENTS

The research and photography for this book received the support and co-operation of a vast number of people. Nevertheless, the assistance of individuals stands out and particular thanks are due to the Minister of Information of the State of Bahrain. H. E. Tariq Almoayed, who from the outset gave full encouragement to the project and made available the facilities of the Ministry of Information to arrange appointments and photographic permissions. Ahmed Al Sherooqi and Mustafa Al Khatib proved never failing with their friendly advice and comprehensive knowledge. Mohammed Al Sayegh was a constant and understanding companion during my travels around Bahrain. Many organisations lent their support, notably the Ministry of Education, the Gulf Polytechnic, the Bahrain Museum, the Coast Guard, Bahrain Bankers Training Centre, ALBA, ASRY, BAPCO, BATELCO and above all the Department of Heritage whose director, Shaikha Nayla Al Khalifa kindly supplied many of the black-and-white prints which appear in this book from the extensive collection of historical material which she has compiled as a record of Bahrain's heritage. The India Office in London were painstaking in tracking down historical maps of Bahrain. Michael Rice gave valuable advice on the manuscript. Nevertheless, any errors in fact or judgement are my own.

Finally, I owe a debt of gratitude to the people of Bahrain whose warmth and friendliness were a vital support and encouragement and turned the making of this book into a memorable and rewarding experience. I have attempted to reflect something of Bahrain's people today as well as of their history and it is my hope that Bahrainis will find this a worthy account of themselves and of their national heritage.

The Publishers wish to acknowledge grateful thanks to the British Museum for their kind permission to reproduce copyright material on pages vi, xvi.

The minarets of the Al Khamis Mosque

INTRODUCTION

The title "Bahrain: Gulf Heritage in Transition" may be over-ambitious in that the subject matter is, after all, Bahrain itself. Nevertheless, it stands as a reminder that Bahrain needs to be understood within the context of the Gulf and that the forces at work in Bahrain are representative of the region at large.

The phenomenon of transition is of central significance in Bahrain today. It is all too easy for the new arrival to accept at face value the modern developments without a thought for the traditional life which had survived centuries practically unchanged until the oil-age of the twentieth century. Perhaps it would be more appropriate to use the term "oil revolution" as "industrial revolution" is used to describe a process which has changed society and the environment in such a radical manner. The taxi driver who takes you from the airport to one of the luxury hotels might be a retired pearl-diver and his son a student of computer technology in California. That, in an extreme example, is the sort of developmental progress to be encountered. And the luxury hotels did not exist ten years ago, and neither did the land on which they are constructed, for it was yet to be reclaimed from the sea.

Many of the people the visitor meets are not from Bahrain. According to the 1981 census, 112,378 of the total population of 350,798 were non-Bahraini, that is, one third of the present inhabitants are in a sense a temporary phenomenon, most of them serving two or three years before moving on. There is thus a dimension of transience to be added to that of transition; not forgetting the endless stream of emissaries, salesmen and "experts" whose brief stays on the island are reported in the local media to be fixed momentarily in the public awareness before they move on as the nomads of the modern age.

For all these, there is not room in this book which concentrates on the people of Bahrain themselves. The first part is retrospective, tracing the development of the islands through the ages in order to cast light on the heritage of Bahrain. The photographs of the second part show Bahrainis, young and old, in new and traditional situations. The habitat is shown at its most extreme forms in order to contrast the heritage of the past with the futuristic scene of today. Whereas fifty years ago the population was predominantly rural, the percentage now living in urban areas has risen above eighty per cent. The final part is by way of an afterword to outline the major developmental forces at work and with brief reference to the regional picture. The general aim is to open a window on Bahrain in words and pictures and to present some of the human and physical reality which is often missing in the political and economic analyses.

Dhow builder's yard

Part One

BAHRAIN THROUGH THE AGES

Until about the middle of this present century the standard work of reference on the region of the Gulf was the formidable four-volume *Gazetteer of the Persian Gulf*[1] by J. G. Lorimer of the Indian Civil Service published in 1915 at Calcutta. The section on the history of Bahrain begins: "In tracing the course of events in Bahrain it is unnecessary to go back beyond 1602 about which year the Portuguese were expelled from the islands . . ."

In fairness to Lorimer – who was in any case writing a handbook for imperial administrators – the facts of Bahrain's early history had not yet been properly investigated. Awaiting rediscovery were some three millennia of a previous existence as one of the great independent trading nations. There was, however, plenty of speculation – based mainly on the burial mounds, estimated variously between one hundred and two hundred thousand in number – as to the truth about life on Bahrain in the far distant past.

The first serious investigation into the tumuli on record was by another British civil servant, Captain E. L. Durand whose report *The Antiquities of Bahrain* was published in 1880. Durand's account is concerned with many aspects of Bahrain and the "antiquities" as such receive only cursory attention. Like others who were to follow, Durand was firmly convinced of a Phoenician connection: "It will however scarcely be called in question that these

islands of Bahrain were in old days inhabited by a Phoenician race and that they had here temples to their gods." This view was based on a statement by the Greek historian Herodotus that the Phoenicians believed that they originated from the Gulf. Yet it was the origin of the tumuli which above all else preoccupied Durand: "Only one puzzle remains. If these miles upon miles of crowded heaps are tombs, where did the inhabitants live?" The idea of Bahrain as a vast regional burial ground seems to have caught the romantic imagination and asserted itself against other possibilities. Durand goes on to speculate: "May not some ancient tribe of Phoenicians on the mainland have looked to sleep their long sleep in the hallowed dust of these sacred islands? This may seem a far-fetched idea, but the vastness of the series of mounds must be my excuse. I have not heard of such another necropolis above ground in the world."

At any event the "long sleep" was about to be broken and the "hallowed dust" scattered as Durand commenced investigation of some of the largest mounds near the village of A'ali, using methods more appropriate to road building than to archaeological excavation. With crowbars, pick-axes and finally gunpowder he forced his way in, unfortunately causing damage to the mounds in the process so that the value of his "sondage" was almost negligible.

Yet Durand's visit was a momentous step forward in the uncovering of Bahrain's early history. He was told of a stone that nobody could read and he succeeded in tracing it to the "holy of holies" in a mosque near the village of Bilad al Qadim where it

---

[1] "Persian Gulf". . . now known as the "Arabian Gulf" or simply "The Gulf". In fact the Gulf has traditionally been an Arab lake since the sailors and fishermen on both sides are mainly of Arab stock.

The burial mounds near A'ali prompted the first efforts to uncover the secrets of Bahrain's early past

was embedded in a wall. Durand negotiated the purchase of the stone for "a few rupees" and had it removed. He thus took away with him a crucial piece of evidence which was to establish Bahrain's identity as Dilmun, a maritime trading power mentioned frequently on the clay tablets being excavated in Mesopotamia at that time.

Durand's stone was a basalt block bearing a cuneiform inscription dating back to about 2000 BC:

"Palace of Rimum, servant of the god Inzak, man of Agarum." Its discovery was notified to Sir Henry Rawlinson who was deciphering some of the thousands of tablets from Mesopotamia, and it chanced that he had encountered Inzak as the principal deity of Dilmun. Thus it was that the eminent Assyriologist, Sir Henry Rawlinson, was the first to suggest, in his report on the Durand report of 1880, that the location of Dilmun was Bahrain.

The re-emergence of Dilmun into the mainstream of history passed almost unnoticed at the time, possibly because so little was known about Dilmun and more spectacular discoveries were being brought to the attention of the public. The Durand stone, having resurfaced after almost four thousand years of oblivion, was not even housed in a museum but remained in private hands and eventually disappeared, presumed destroyed during an air raid in the last war. Although its significance had been understood and committed to record by one of the greatest authorities of the day, the implications of this piece of evidence to identify Bahrain with Dilmun were to await proper evaluation until the 1950s.

The intrepid Arabian travellers, Theodore and Mabel Bent, who visited Bahrain in 1889 on the first leg of their epic journey described in their book *Southern Arabia* were as taken with the Phoenician connection as was Durand and no mention is made of Dilmun. Following in the footsteps of their predecessor, the Bents excavated two mounds near A'ali: "As we ourselves brought to light objects of distinctly Phoenician origin, there would appear to be no longer any room for doubt that the mounds which lay before us were a vast necropolis of this mercantile race." So wrote Mabel and proceeded to conclusions less romantic than those of Durand ten years earlier: ". . . one of two suppositions must be correct, either firstly, that the Phoenicians originally lived here before they migrated to the Mediterranean . . . or secondly, that these islands were looked upon by them as a sacred spot for the burial of their dead . . . I am much more inclined to the former supposition, judging from the mercantile importance of the Bahrain Islands and the excellent school they must have been for a race which was to penetrate all the then known corners of the globe . . ."

Fascination with the Phoenician theory also influenced the thinking of Colonel Prideaux who tackled eight of the largest mounds in the vicinity of A'ali in 1906. Ernest Mackay, sent in 1925 by the great archaeologist Flinders Petrie, opened nearly fifty mounds, but the results were disappointing since all the graves had previously been plundered. Mackay postulated, using slender evidence, that Bahrain was not even inhabited at the time of the construction of the tumuli, and he came out in support of the hypothesis of Durand that Bahrain was an enormous island cemetery for a population based on the mainland of the Arabian Peninsula.

The aura of mystery around the Phoenician question and the necropolis theory lingered on to divert attention from other avenues of investigation into the early history of Bahrain. More information about Dilmun was yet emerging as the work of deciphering tablets discovered in Mesopotamia progressed. The original hoard of twenty-five thousand tablets from the palace at Nineveh which had been brought to light in 1839 and the thirty to forty thousand tablets from the University of Pennsylvania's expeditions to Nippur, commencing in 1888/9, contained the essential elements of Sumerian mythology and several significant references to the role which Dilmun played within it. A Sumerian version of the flood, published in 1914, featured Dilmun as a place of immortality, the eternal home of the ancestor of all mankind:

"Anu and Enlil cherished Ziusudra, life like a god they give him, breath eternal like a god they bring down for him. Then Ziusudra the king, the preserver of the name of vegetation and of the seed of mankind, in the land of the crossing, the land of Dilmun, the place where the sun rises, they caused to dwell."

In another famous text from Nippur, first published in 1915 and re-translated in 1945, we encounter Dilmun as a land of spiritual purity:

"The holy cities – present them to him,
The land of Dilmun is holy.
Holy Sumer – present it to him,
the land of Dilmun is holy.
The land of Dilmun is holy, the land of Dilmun
    is pure,
the land of Dilmun is clean, the land of Dilmun
    is holy."

The repetition of the key phrase evokes the mood of a religious incantation but elsewhere the poetry is full of strong images:

Cross section of an excavated burial mound near A'ali revealing the central chamber

"In Dilmun the raven utters no cry,
the wild hen utters not the cry of the wild hen,
the lion kills not,
the wolf snatches not the lamb,
unknown is the kid-devouring wild dog,
unknown is the grain-devouring boar.
The malt which the widow spreads on the
roof –
the birds of heaven do not eat up that malt.
The dove droops not the head.
The sick-eyed says not 'I am sick-eyed',
the sick-headed says not 'I am sick-headed',
its old woman says not 'I am an old woman',
its old man says not 'I am an old man.'"

This beguiling vision of paradise would seem to refer to a place of the imagination rather than of actual fact and make Dilmun appear a product of mythological fantasy rather than a geographical reality. Not so the following passage which mentions physical attributes of Dilmun:

"Let Utu stationed in heaven
bring you sweet water from the earth,
from the water sources of the earth;
let him bring up the water into your large
    reservoirs;
let him take your city drink from them the
    water of abundance;
let him make Dilmun drink from them the
    water of abundance;
let your wells of bitter water become wells of
    sweet water;
let your furrowed fields and acres yield you
    their grain·
let your city become the 'dockyard' – house of
    the land."

Perhaps the reservoirs are more appropriate to parts of Mesopotamia than to a land blessed with a constant supply of underground water, but in other respects the description sounds real enough. Thus Dilmun straddles the realms of myth and fact. As the series of Danish expeditions between 1953 and 1965 were later to suggest, Sumerian mythology and its belief in a world below of sweet water coincide with the physical aspects of Bahrain's geography.

However, rather than pre-empt the possibilities raised by the Danish excavation of the Barbar temple, which will be discussed in their place, it is as well to leave the mythology of Dilmun for the time being.

The Dilmun of fact, partly overlapping with the poetry of legend, offered equal mystery to the investigators. Until the nineteenth-century discovery of the clay tablets in Mesopotamia, Dilmun had been a lost civilisation. Its very name had slipped from the conscious knowledge of mankind over a period of almost 2,500 years and yet, as the tablets and further excavations revealed, Dilmun played the essential role in the flourishing trade between the ancient civilisations of the Indus Valley and of Mesopotamia. The first-ever reference to Dilmun coincides with the beginning of civilisation in Mesopotamia in the fourth millennium. Thus the traders of Dilmun were at the centre of the first commerce of the ancient world and left their traces from the eastern Mediterranean to the shores of India. At the time of its glory Dilmun must have been in the vanguard of civilisation with its name enhanced by the romance of mythology.

Sargon of Assyria, recording his military campaigns in the eighth century BC, reported that he had reached the borders of Dilmun:
"Uperi, king of Dilmun, whose abode is situated, like a fish, thirty double-hours away in the midst of the sea of the rising sun, heard of the might of my sovereignty and sent his gifts."

This conciliatory gesture rings true of an independent trading power whose prosperity flowed from the commerce between mightier neighbours. Dilmun must have been aware of the ways of superpowers for it is also recorded that King Sargon of Akkad in c. 2300 BC had conquered all the territory between the Mediterranean and the Gulf, including Dilmun itself which probably encompassed not only the islands of Bahrain but most of the coast of Arabia as well.

Dilmun's prosperity came from a happy combination of natural and economic factors. The islands were blessed with an excellent water supply, capable of sustaining a rich and diverse agriculture and surrounded by a sea abundant in fish and yielding pearls which are described in the tablets of the early second millennium as "fish-eyes". These advantages were crowned by a strategic location astride the main trade routes between the world's first empires in the valleys of the Tigris and Euphrates and their sources of supply across the waters of the Gulf and the Arabian Sea.

Details of that rich commerce came to light in tablets discovered at Ur in 1930/31 by Sir Leonard Woolley. File copies of the business correspondence on clay tablets of the Dilmun-trader, a certain Ea-nasir, between 1813 BC and 1790 BC indicated that the main item of that trade was copper. The copper originated from another lost kingdom, that of Makan now considered to have been located in the ore-rich

The "Dilmun City" site near the Bahrain Fort. A high standard of masonry is evident

mountains of the area presently occupied by the Sultanate of Oman.

If copper was the mainstay of Dilmun's trade it was handsomely supplemented by the transit in luxury goods and materials from the Indus Valley. Gold, ivory, tortoise-shell, carnelian, lapis-lazuli, coral, precious woods, even eye-paint for the ladies of Ur and Nineveh passed through Dilmun where the ready availability of sweet water made it the natural point of convergence for the trading fleets which sailed the Gulf between the mouth of the Euphrates, the Indus and the coast of Oman.

The wealth and diversity of Dilmun's trade was such that it was celebrated in verse, as witnessed by further tablets discovered at Ur:

> "May the land Tukrish transport to you gold from Harali, lapis lazuli, . . .;
> May the land Meluhha bring you tempting precious carnelian, mes-shagan wood, fine sea-wood, sailors;
> May the land Marhashi bring you precious stone, crystal;
> May the land Magan bring you mighty copper, the strength of . . ., diorite, u-stone, shuman-stone;
> May the Sealand transport to you ebony, the . . . ornament of the king,
> May the land Zalamgar transport to you wool, good ore, . . .;
> May the land Elam transport to you . . . wool, tribute;
> May the shrine Ur, the daïs of kingship, the . . . city, transport to you grain, sesame-oil, noble garments, fine garments, sailors;
> May the wide sea bring you its abundance.
> The city – its dwellings are good dwellings,
> Dilmun – its dwellings are good dwellings, . . ."

This amazingly detailed inventory of Dilmun's transit trade indicates a counter-flow from the north of such commodities as wool, clothing, grain and sesame-oil as well as tribute. The two references to sailors suggest that Dilmun's fleets included manpower from Meluhha (Indus?) and from Ur. Clearly this was no minor trading nation for the wealth of

The "Absu" at the re-excavated Barbar Temple where the sweet water of the world below comes to the surface

Dilmun had been sufficient to finance the development of a city with "good dwellings"; and it was the dwellings of Dilmun, its palaces and temples, which were the objective of the series of archaeological expeditions organised by the University of Aarhus in Denmark from 1953 to 1965. For if Bahrain were in truth Dilmun then something must remain of the human habitations set up over a period of more than two millennia of prosperous civilisation. This switch of emphasis from the burial mounds to urban settlements proved to be a decisive breakthrough in the investigation of Bahrain's early past.

The full account of the rediscovery of Dilmun, as given by the expedition organiser Geoffrey Bibby in *Looking for Dilmun*, has the excitement of a detective story. It unravels not only the essential threads of Bahrain's Dilmun period but places it in relation to the wider regional picture. Working from two main sites, the early Dilmun city partially covered by the Portuguese Fort, or Qalat al Bahrain, and the Bronze Age temples near the village of Barbar, the Danes followed a trail of clues which led them north to Failaka off Kuwait, south to Qatar, Abu Dhabi and Oman, and also to the neighbouring coastal zone of Saudi Arabia.

In addition to the circumstantial evidence provided by Sumerian legend, the business correspondence from Ur and the mysteriously-vanished Durand stone, came the first physical evidence to be found on Bahrain that this was in fact the trading and administrative centre of Dilmun. The discovery of merchants' seals and even the tools of a seal-maker were just what was needed. Distinctive as an authentic product of Dilmun/Bahrain, identical seals had been discovered at Ur and in the Indus Valley, dating from the second millennium. These seals, related to yet different from those originating in Mesopotamia and the Indus Valley, had to be assumed to come from Dilmun even without exact knowledge of Dilmun's location. Positive identification of their place of origin helped to authenticate Bahrain's role as Dilmun. Work on the Qalat al Bahrain site established the early chronology of Dilmun, but as Bibby freely admits: ". . . the areas we dug were too small to give us a picture of the life of the city at any one time." The scope for future investigation becomes evident when one considers another statement in *Looking for Dilmun*: ". . . this tell (Qalat al Bahrain) was no small town. With an area of almost 40 acres it was a city that could bear comparison with the larger cities of Mesopotamia".

Meanwhile the excavation of the temple site at Barbar had revealed a building of major religious significance where the spring water from the well and the temple pool formed a central element in the design. This caused Bibby to reflect on the Sumerian belief that both the earth and the salt sea of the physical environment rested upon another sea called the "absu" or the "abyss". Enki, the lord of the sweet water under the earth in the "Epic of Gilgamesh", occupied a significant place in the mythology of the time both as a creator and a benefactor of mankind. Clearly, a place where the sweet waters of the deep rose up through the salt water of the sea would enjoy special status. The abundant wells and submarine springs of Bahrain would have had religious significance for the people of Mesopotamia, who believed furthermore that at the beginning of the world the gods dwelled mainly in Dilmun, which they had blessed with sweet water, vegetation, health and eternal youth. This combination of factors and the discovery of the temple well led Bibby to speculate: "To the Sumerians, and probably even more to the people of Dilmun, such a spring was not a natural phenomenon. Here were the waters of the Abyss, here the sweet waters of the sea-beneath-the-world broke through to the surface. This might be the very spring which Enki, the Lord of the Abyss, had caused to gush forth in Dilmun, at the behest of the goddess Ninsikilla."

Another interesting aspect of the famous sweet water springs of Bahrain (which in Arabic means "the two seas") is the local Arab legend reported by Durand according to which they had their source in an underground river still running from the Euphrates. A further link between the reality of Bahrain and the mythological epic of Gilgamesh is suggested by the fact that the instructions given to Gilgamesh in order to achieve his quest for immortality required him "to attach stones to his feet, and by their aid sink down to the bed of the sea, and there pluck the magic flower." This is an exact description of the technique of the Bahraini pearl-divers from the third millennium until the middle of the twentieth century. In spite of such tantalising circumstantial evidence, Bibby freely admits to have entered the realm of speculation by suggesting that Gilgamesh came to Bahrain. The positive identification of Bahrain as Dilmun will, however, only be questioned by those requiring such absolute proof as an inscription stating that this, Bahrain, is Dilmun.

The Danish expeditions made less spectacular progress on the original cause of the interest in Bahrain's prehistoric past, the burial mounds. It was postulated that the temple at Barbar, the Dilmun "City II" at Qalat al Bahrain, and most of the gravemounds were all of the Early Dilmun Period (2300–1750 BC) and that during the Middle Dilmun Period (1750–1259 BC) and the late Dilmun Period, which extended to c. 500 BC, none were built. The

practice appears to have been resumed for a century or so during the Seleucid Period (300–0 BC). However, there is now some questioning of this chronology. Furthermore, the connection between the tumuli and the known facts of Dilmun remains unclear and the question posed by Captain Durand, Theodore and Mabel Bent, Colonel Prideaux and others as to whether Bahrain served as a regional necropolis is unresolved. The documentary film made to narrate the tale of the Danish excavations was purposely entitled *Land of the Living* in order to dispel notions of Bahrain as "an island of the dead". Yet the existence of the world's largest prehistoric burial ground will continue to fuel speculation and it is not altogether inconceivable that a thriving commerce and a thriving burial cult were contemporaneous, if separate, elements of Dilmun civilisation.

The picture that emerges of Bahrain in the Dilmun period is an outline lacking in intimate detail. From the available evidence we can imagine an industrious population, rich through agriculture and international trade. Large numbers were probably employed in the date gardens and the fishing fleets. Pearling was already developed in the third millennium. The boat-building industry would have played an important role. Although the copper kingdom of Makan and the cities of the Indus Valley could finance their own merchant fleets, Dilmun probably offered repair facilities as well as yards for constructing its own vessels from imported wood. We can assume a caste of priests and kings guiding the affairs of state but a merchant class must have formed the backbone of society. Although no accounts or business correspondence have been found in Bahrain, a high degree of literacy and numeracy were required to conduct the large volume of trade indicated by the records of the Dilmun clients living in Mesopotamia. It is known that the merchants of Dilmun adopted the weights and measures of the Indus Valley, and from the merchants' correspondence found in Ur it appears that a banking system with letters of credit and guarantees was in existence, regulated perhaps by an embryonic chamber of commerce. Indeed, it is the proven commercial acumen of Dilmun, linked to the navigational skills of the merchant fleet, which continues to suggest an association with the Phoenicians.

Little is known of the circumstances of Dilmun's decline but it can be ascribed to the shifting economic and political scene in the Middle East in the course of the first millennium BC. Dilmun had always been susceptible to upheavals in the region which disturbed or interrupted trade, such as the Aryan destruction of the Indus Valley cities which, it is suggested, cut off the supply of goods at some period between 1800 and 1600 BC. In spite of continual struggles between rival powers in Mesopotamia trade managed to hold up. Dilmun was prosperous enough to attract the Babylonians shortly after 600 BC and to be incorporated into their empire with provincial status. In 538 BC Babylonia was conquered by the Persians, and Dilmun became part of the Persian Empire which extended from India to the Mediterranean. Doubtless the new political configuration offered attractive trading possibilities for the islands of Bahrain well into the Seleucid Period (300–0 BC) and the ensuing Parthian Period (0–AD 300) but external factors suggest that the boom years were over.

With the rise of the Greeks and the growing economic might of the Eastern Mediterranean, the Indian trade had found an alternative route through the Red Sea. In addition, the mariners of southern Arabia, that is, present-day Yemen and Oman, had mastered the monsoon winds and were trading independently with India. This maritime commerce was able to connect up with the overland routes of the incense caravans. By the middle of the first millennium BC the south Arabian kingdoms of Hadramaut, Qataban, Saba and Ma'in were taking over the role of commercial middleman once held exclusively by Dilmun. During the next thousand years the desert highway or incense route via the now forsaken cities of Shabwa, Timna, Marib and Baraqish, on the way north to the Mediterranean at Gaza, was the golden road for international trade. Dilmun was relegated to a regional role. Archaeological evidence – or rather the lack of it – would appear to confirm a fall in prosperity. The pottery samples from the Dilmun city at Qalat al Bahrain show a gap of over a thousand years

between the Attic ware (not later than 200 BC) and the next phase of Chinese celadon (not earlier than AD 900). This anomaly does not of course mean that the islands of Bahrain were uninhabited during this period but that the sophisticated city culture of Dilmun had perhaps passed away.

Until the coming of Islam in the seventh century AD several centuries came and went without leaving any archaeological traces. The traditional date cultivation, pearling and fishing required no more than "barasti" villages, which, unlike the earlier palaces, have left behind neither piles of rubble nor signs of foundations. Knowledge of this period is scanty.

One can assume from the outline of external events in the region that the islands of Bahrain were for much of the time under the domination of Arab tribes from the mainland, which even ventured to carry out raids within Persia. One such, in the fourth century AD, brought retribution from the Sassanid king Shapur II who annexed eastern Arabia and Bahrain. What this annexation meant in real terms to the inhabitants of Bahrain is difficult to assess. Apparently Shapur placed his new acquisitions under the authority of the King of Hira, an Arab buffer state on the south-west border of Sassanid Persia. So Bahrain, although nominally under Persian overlordship, was still under Arab management. Probably the foreign politics of the period had little effect on the details of everyday life in Bahrain at this time. Date cultivation, fishing and pearling – supplemented by local handicrafts — continued to be the support of the population which, just prior to the revelation of Islam in the seventh century, was reported by later mediaeval Arab chroniclers to consist of Abd al Qais tribes who also inhabited the oases and coastal districts of eastern Arabia.

According to Spencer Trimingham in his study *Christianity Among the Arabs in Pre-Islamic Times*, the Abd al Qais were Christians at the time of the Prophet and find mention in the annals of Islam. The King of Hira was an adherent to Nestorianism and there were a number of Nestorian bishops in the Gulf region, including one in Bahrain. From other sources we learn, however, that Christianity was not the dominant religion in Bahrain at the time of the introduction of Islam. Pagan Arabs, Jews, Zoroastrians, as well as Christians, were all to be found in the region of Bahrain. Yaqut, an Arab chronicler of the thirteenth century, confirms that the name Bahrain denoted at the time: ". . . a region that occupies the coastal area on the Indian Sea (the Gulf) between Basra and Oman." Thus it is often not possible to distinguish between comments relating to the islands of Bahrain and those concerning the region as a whole. Sometimes the principal island of Bahrain is mentioned specifically as Uwal or Awal.

Whatever unclarity may exist about conditions in Bahrain in the immediate pre-Islamic period there is no doubt that the incorporation of Bahrain into the world community of Islam was an event of fundamental and enduring significance. Since Islam encompasses not only religious but also social, legal and economic principles it creates within the community of Islamic nations a system of shared values. No matter what divisions appear above or beneath the surface of politics there remains a constant underlying urge to achieve a harmonisation of interests. With the embracing of Islam in the seventh century, Bahrain became a member of the world community based on spiritual values which was soon to extend from south-east Asia to Spain. Although the aspired unity of Islam foundered as old political rivalries were often continued in the guise of religious issues, the unifying forces of Islam over the centuries in the long run outweighed the elements of disunity. Adherence to Islam added a new dimension to Bahrain's polity. The glory of Dilmun's commercial and mythological golden age was certainly over and the emerging

Inscription from the foundation stone marking the reconstruction of the Al Khamis Mosque. 16th Century. Bahrain Museum

Islamic state had little prospect of great material success, yet the new religion, culture and social system created the framework within which the subsequent development of Bahrain has happened. The Islamic and Arab heritage contains the essential elements of Bahrain's identity which have been transmitted through fourteen centuries of a national development that has repeatedly been influenced by external forces.

At the centre of the struggle within the Islamic world power went to the tough and talented Umayyad princes, who gave their name to the first dynasty within the Islamic Caliphate which ruled from Damascus from 661 to 750 AD. This was the period of the great Islamic expansion, an almost spontaneous outburst of conquering zeal which eventually outran the forces necessary to sustain it from within. Bahrain's political and commercial position were at this time rendered marginal to the mainstream of life within the region which focussed on the wonders emanating from the Umayyad seat of power in Damascus.

The subsequent transfer of power to the Abbasids in Baghdad benefited Bahrain's trade, which was traditionally geared to Mesopotamia, but politically the islands remained dependencies of the central authority of the Caliphate. For short periods they were used as a stronghold and refuge by schismatic groups opposed to the Abbasids. In spite of these minor revolts the Abbasid Caliphs maintained control over Bahrain from 750 to 899 AD, and the allegiance of the islands was to Baghdad.

This was broken by the ascendancy of an extreme Ismaili sect which established a power-base in eastern Arabia. The Carmathians or Caramites were one of the most obscure and controversial movements to emerge throughout the entire span of Islamic history. They established themselves in Bahrain, then known as Awal, during the tenth and for half of the eleventh century. Their record of government, as summarised in Bahrain's historical revue *Al Watheeka* (Number 1 – July 1982) appears questionable: "Though originating from the Ismailis, the Caramites geared themselves to launching a campaign against the Abbasids, the Ismailis and the Fatimids altogether. Their leaders raised the

One of the twin minarets of the Al Khamis Mosque which has become a landmark in Bahrain

slogan of social justice and talked of building an ideal society, but ended up by practising terrorism, murder, tyranny and oppression. The ideologues of the Caramites began by having recourse to intellect and logic but soon deteriorated into practitioners of superstition, astrology and personality cult. However, the beginning of the end came on the Island of Awal where Abil-Bahloul sealed the fate of one of the

— 13 —

most bigoted and harsh groups in Islamic history." Thus Bahrain had early and direct experience of the reality of the ideal revolutionary society.

Abil-Bahloul broke the power of the Caramites, but he in turn was defeated by the Ayunis, Arab tribes of al Ahsa in eastern Arabia who ruled over the region including Bahrain for the next two hundred years. Al Idrisi gave a description of life on Bahrain in 1154 which mentions agriculture, pearling, fresh-water springs as well as the administration: "The island is governed by an independent chief. The inhabitants of the two banks are satisfied with his justice and his piety, and when he dies he is replaced by a person who equals him in virtue and justice." Elsewhere we learn, however, that Bahrain still recognised the authority of the Caliph at Baghdad to whom tribute was sent.

There is a thirteenth-century description by Ibn al Mujawir who states that the people of Bahrain are Arabs, and that there are 360 villages. The famous fourteenth-century Arab traveller, Ibn Battuta, vis-ited Bahrain in about 1332 and left a highly vivid, if somewhat inaccurate, account of the pearl-divers: "Before diving the diver puts on his face a sort of tortoiseshell mask and a tortoiseshell clip on his nose, then he ties a rope round his waist and dives. They differ in their endurance under water, some of them being able to stay under for an hour or two hours or less. When he reaches the bottom of the sea he finds the shells there stuck in the sand between small stones, and pulls them out by hand or cuts them loose with a knife which he has for the purpose, and puts them in a leather bag slung round his neck. When his breath becomes restricted he pulls the rope, and the man holding the rope on the shore feels the movement and pulls him up into the boat. The bag is taken from him and the shells are opened. Inside them are found pieces of flesh which are cut out with a knife, and when they come into contact with the air solidify and turn into pearls. These are then collected, large and small together; the sultan takes his fifth and the remainder are bought by the merchants who are there in the boats. Most of them are the creditors of the divers, and they take the pearls in quittance of their debt or so much of it as is their due."

Ibn Battuta's description of Bahrain is brief. He refers to "a fine large town with orchards, trees and streams. Water is easy to get at there; all one has to do is to scoop the ground with one's hands. It is very hot and sandy, and the sand often encroaches on some of its settlements."

During the fourteenth century Bahrain witnessed many changes of ruler, with the islands eventually passing from the direct control of Hormuz to a brief spell of relative independence in union with Qatif and Hasa under Shaikh Ibrahim al Maliki during the fifteenth century. Soon, however, a new power entered the arena of the Gulf and substantially raised the stakes in the constant struggle for territorial supremacy. At the beginning of the sixteenth cen-tury, with the advent of the Portuguese, Bahrain encountered a new breed of merchant traders intent on dominating the Indian trade, once the preserve of ancient Dilmun.

Seen in retrospect, Bahrain's first seven centuries under the banner of Islam involved the islands in the wider political developments of the time. The destiny of Bahrain was henceforth intimately linked to the mainland of the Arabian Peninsula. Bahrain's popu-lation at the time – as has been confirmed by recent linguistic evidence – belonged to the ancient eastern Arabian tribes and at various times there was a common rule as well as common blood.

Archaeological evidence of early Islam in Bahrain is confined to a few sites. The earliest mosque at Suq al Khamis has been ascribed to the tenth or the eleventh century AD. Inscriptions reveal that the mosque in its definitive form was built in the fourteenth century and was partially rebuilt in the fifteenth. The two imposing minarets are of mediaeval construction and recently restored. Var-ious inscriptions from the Caramite period have been found, but these do not give a picture of life at the time.

It is evident, however, that the principal sites occupied in the Dilmun Period had been abandoned and that the well at Barbar no longer enjoyed any special religious significance. Islamic civilisation in Bahrain appears to have regrouped around the famous springs and pools of Ain Qasari and Ain Adari in the vicinity of Khamis and Bilad al Qadim.

The sweet water spring at Ain Adari came into prominence in the Islamic period. The site is today the focal point of a national park

The tell left behind by the ruins of the Dilmun city served as the foundation for a fort which did not deter successive raids and invasions. The mention of 360 villages in the thirteenth century does not necessarily indicate a high level of population and prosperity but perhaps a scattered population dwelling in small tribal units and living off the produce of the land and the sea. Manamah – literally the "place of sleep" – was first mentioned around 1330 AD when Turan Shah of Hormuz visited the island. The name does not suggest the activity of a busy administrative or commercial centre but conjures up a pleasant image of rest in the shady groves of Ras Rumman, or "Pomegranate Head", as the promontory of old Manamah was called. Whatever reality lay behind the "place of sleep", the thunder of Portuguese cannon blasted Bahrain from its mediaeval slumber at the beginning of the sixteenth century.

The Portuguese had devoted themselves to the discovery of a direct route to India and the East, well aware of the great profit which would result from wresting from the Middle East its monopoly as middle-man in the trade between Europe and Asia. Finally, in 1498, Vasco da Gama reached India via the Cape and opened a new chapter of history in the region. Henceforth, the Portuguese kings styled themselves: "Lords of the Conquest, Navigation and Commerce of India, Ethiopia, Arabia and Persia".

Under the formidable Alfonso de Albuquerque, later to be appointed Viceroy of Portuguese India, Hormuz was conquered and transformed into a Portuguese base. Bahrain at the time owed allegiance to the King of Hormuz and in due course received a visit of inspection in 1514 from the great Albuqerque who confirmed the existing treaties. The relationship with the Portuguese was subsequently repudiated by Mukarram, King of Hasa, who invaded the islands in 1521. This brought retribution from the Portuguese who launched a counter-invasion.

From this event dates the formal Portuguese occupation of Bahrain which lasted until 1602. It is extremely unlikely that the Portuguese tried to use in Bahrain the coercive methods of conversion to Christianity so ruthlessly applied in their Indian

possession of Goa. Probably they sensed the moral outrage and rebellion which such tactics would bring in a solidly Muslim country. As it was, the inhabitants of Bahrain found the Portuguese presence irksome enough to rise up, murder the hated governor and reclaim their independence. The leader of the revolt, Hussein bin Sa'id, eventually came to terms with the Portuguese and accepted their adviser. Yet in 1529 came another serious challenge to Portuguese authority. In 1534 there is record of independent rulers of Bahrain and Hasa sending envoys to Iraq to greet the Turkish Sultan, Suleiman the Magnificent, after the Ottomans had assumed the Islamic Caliphate at the beginning of the sixteenth century. This token of respect did not deter the Turks from attacking Bahrain in 1559, when it was the turn of the Portuguese to come to the rescue of their governor and the islands. The final collapse of Portuguese rule in Bahrain came in 1602 when the governor crowned a most tyrannical rule by the murder of a leading Bahraini merchant in order to obtain his wealth. The foul deed was avenged by the brother of the dead man, who not only killed the Portuguese governor but also launched a successful attack against the fort. Bahrain then invoked Persian protection to stave off a counter-attack and the Portuguese schemes to regain possession of Bahrain were effectively thwarted.

Apart from the fort, little remains of the Portuguese occupation of Bahrain. There is no trace of any churches such as those constructed so liberally in Goa; but in a sense the fort tells the whole tale. Within it an insecure Portuguese garrison kept watch for an invasion from the sea but always with a wary eye to rebellion and assault from Bahrain itself. Relations with the inhabitants were generally not of a cordial nature and the Portuguese did not have a lasting influence on the heritage of Bahrain. It is not without irony that the Portuguese names such as Mendez, Fernandez, Braganza and many others which failed to take root in the sixteenth century in Bahrain can now be encountered there in abundance as a result of recent immigration from Goa.

The Portuguese lingered on in the Gulf for more than a century after the loss of Bahrain, but theirs

Looking out from within the Portuguese Fort, also known as the Bahrain Fort since there is evidence of an earlier Islamic fortification on the site

*Arad Fort on the island of Muharraq. An Omani construction on a
Portuguese foundation testifies to a turbulent period in the history of Bahrain*

was an increasingly hopeless cause. The Dutch and the English in varying coalitions with the Persians conspired to out-manoeuvre them. In the first half of the seventeenth century it appeared that the Dutch might emerge as the dominant foreign power in the region, but their losses on the European front weakened their position in the East. It was the English who became masters of the Persian trade and the first English "factories" or trading stations date back to around 1616/17.

Although Persia became the base of the East India Company's operations, Bahrain was seriously considered as an alternative. Thomas Aldworth's report of 1613: "I find there is a seaport called Bareyn, whereunto a ship of 2 or 3 hundred tons may come, and I understand this country spends much cloth, for the Venetians bring it overland and

so carry with them again all sorts of Persian silks, which trade is, as it were, offered us, and surely I think in short time will be able to vent as much cloth as Surat." However, Bahrain was passed over, reconsidered in 1752, but the East India Company eventually settled on establishing their Gulf headquarters in Bushire on the Persian side.

After the Portuguese withdrawal in 1602 Bahrain was under the control of a series of Persian governors until the end of the seventeenth century. In 1718 a shock Omani invasion caused such distress and suffering that the unwelcome occupation and oppression was only brought to an end by "the voluntary removal from their homes of the indigenous population, who emigrated to other places . . ." (Lorimer: *Gazeteer*, op cit.) The Persians ended the unhappy situation by paying off the

Omanis, but a period of extreme turbulence then ensued as independent sheikhdoms, Hawala Arabs, Persians and Omanis alternately disputed the territory. The Omanis launched a major invasion in 1738. In the 1740s Hawala Arabs were in control. In 1753 Sheikh Nasir of Bushire was in possession of the islands of Bahrain.

The effects of the constant upheavals may be assessed from the account of the famous German traveller, Carsten Niebuhr, who visited Bahrain in 1763: "In this isle were once three hundred and sixty towns and villages. At present it contains beside the capital, only sixty wretched villages. A long series of wars have ruined the others."

Niebuhr notes nevertheless: "This isle produces great abundance of dates. But its chief dependence is upon the pearl-fishery, as the best pearls are found here in great abundance. The duties upon the two articles of dates and pearls afford its sovereign a lakh of rupees or 300,000 French livres." There is no mention of trade as such, but some interesting remarks on the origins of the inhabitants: "Our geographers are wrong, as I have elsewhere remarked, in representing a part of Arabia as subject to the monarchs of Persia. So far is it being so, that, on the contrary, the Arabs possess all the sea-coast of the Persian empire, from the mouths of the Euphrates, nearly to those of the Indus." Furthermore: "These settlements upon the coast of Persia belong not, indeed, to Arabia properly so called. But . . . they are independent of Persia, and use the same language, and exhibit the same manners, as the native inhabitants of Arabia." Thus Niebuhr stated in the eighteenth century the case for the "Arabian Gulf".

Internal conditions in Bahrain at this time were troubled. Niebuhr noted: ". . . continual revolutions which take place among this multitude of petty princes." Perhaps this is a somewhat harsh judgement of a European used to more orderly social organisation. In any case both the internal and external affairs of Bahrain were about to be taken in hand.

In 1782 the islands of Bahrain were conquered by the ancestors of the present ruling family, the Al Khalifa, and thereby removed from Persian tutelage.

The Al Khalifa – like their cousins the Al Sabah of Kuwait – were members of the Bani Utbah clan of the 'Anizah confederation of central Arabia, from which the Al Saud family also stems. The Al Khalifa had originally settled in 1716, together with the Al Sabah in Kuwait, and were active in the pearling trade. From 1776 onwards the Al Khalifa moved south to be nearer the pearl banks, establishing themselves in Zubara on the west coast of Qatar, originally a small settlement which they built up into a prosperous trading community. The first contacts between the authorities in Bahrain and the Al Khalifa were friendly, but this did not last. The Persians, in union with their governor in Bahrain, Shaikh Nasr, launched a naval expedition against the Al Khalifa in Zubara. In the aftermath of his victory Sheikh Ahmed al Fatih took possession of Bahrain in the name of the Al Khalifa, who have been the rulers of Bahrain – except for a brief period of Omani occupation (1799–1809) – ever since.

In the initial stages of Al Khalifa rule conditions remained troubled. The Omani occupation had been brought to an end with the assistance of the shock-troops of Islamic fundamentalism, the Wahhabis, whose tough enforcement of their own austere religious standards caused much suffering for the inhabitants of Bahrain. This unhappy period was only terminated by enlisting the help of the governor of Shiraz. Meanwhile the Al Khalifa continued to maintain a presence in Zubara, which sometimes provided a safer haven than Bahrain. Eventually, the entire Al Khalifa community made the definitive move across the water and put down lasting roots in Bahrain.

By 1813 there is once more an encouraging report of life on Bahrain: "Bahrain island is the finest island in the Gulf. It is covered with villages and date gardens; there is a town and a fort of Medina [sic] with 800 or 900 houses. It carries on much trade with Basra and other Gulf ports." (Kennier) However, Bahrain's troubles were not over. The Al Khalifa had to defend their right to the islands against two further determined Omani invasions in 1816 and in 1828. Life for the original inhabitants was made difficult by the re-allocation of resources

Scene from a pearling expedition. Opening the oysters on board after a series of dives

occasioned by the presence of new masters. On the other hand the Al Khalifa actively promoted the trade of Bahrain and quickly re-established the pre-eminence of its merchant fleet in the Gulf. The entire pearl trade of the Gulf was regulated through Bahrain and revenue from pearling paid for an annual import bill from India of an estimated one million rupees.

Accounts of Bahrain's development in the nineteenth century must also point to the broad backcloth of external forces which had such a great influence in the Gulf region. The most crucial factor was the consolidation of British maritime power. The political and military intervention of the British was mainly aimed at providing security for the growing sea traffic with Persia and India, but the campaigns against the pirates of the lower Gulf also sought to suppress the slave trade from Africa. The decisive action was the destruction of the pirates' stronghold at Ras al Khaimah, which was followed by the "General Treaty" of 1820. Although Bahrain was not directly involved in either piracy or the slave trade, its port facilities were used by the pirates who also recruited local manpower and it became a

The renovated fort of Abu Mahur on the island of Muharraq was once a stronghold of the Al Khalifa

signatory of the "General Treaty". Accordingly, a promise was given to abstain from acts of piracy and commerce in slaves at sea.

This first formalisation of an agreement between the Gulf States and Britain marked the beginning of a new internationally-recognised framework of authority. The Arab rulers who were at the time in control of the territories discovered in the British a self-imposed overseer of law and order who could intervene at will and confer or withdraw support, thereby creating international implications affecting the legitimacy of their regimes.

It is not evident that this was the British objective at the outset. In fact, the British initially conducted their affairs through the semi-autonomous East India Company. However, as later events demonstrated, the "General Treaty" of 1820 was the thin end of the wedge. Henceforth, the Gulf rulers had to accommodate increasing demands. For Bahrain this led to the signing of the 1861 "Treaty of Peace and Friendship". On the positive side this gave Bahrain British recognition as an independent state and a solid protection against claims from Persia and Turkey. On the other hand Bahrain was required to abstain from all maritime aggression without British approval.

The policeman's job which Britain had assumed was becoming increasingly complex. In 1867 an outbreak of hostilities caused the British to invoke the promise of non-aggression. By way of a lesson the British – no longer acting through the East India Company but as the Government of India – sent a man-of-war to destroy the Bahraini fleet. By this intervention the British became deeply involved in the internal affairs of the Al Khalifa for they helped put Mohammad bin Khalifa to flight and recognised his brother Ali bin Khalifa as his successor. A period of intense dynastic turmoil ensued before the Al Khalifa family, in 1869, rallied round Shaikh Isa bin Ali, whose reign of fifty-four years created an era of internal stability and firmly consolidated authority in Bahrain.

From about this time at the end of the 1860s Bahrain received several visits from famous travellers who have left us some fascinating insights into life on the islands. W. G. Palgrave, author of *Central and Eastern Arabia*, passed through in 1868. His is a rather sketchy account but not without interest. Of Manamah and Muharraq: "... these two seaports look each other in the face, somewhat like Dover and Calais, though fortunately for them with friendlier feelings, . . . Moharrek is far the prettier of the two to the eye, with its white houses, set off by darker palm-huts, the large low palaces of the Khalifa family, and two or three imposing forts close to the sea-shore. Manamah, though larger in extent than Moharrek,

Shaikh Isa bin Ali, Ruler of Bahrain 1869–1932 portrayed with his sons during the 1920s

has a less showy appearance; it is a centre of commerce, as its vis-a-vis is of government; and hence has fewer palaces to present, and less display of defensive architecture." But, above all, Palgrave delighted in the coffee-houses and harbour activity.

A decade later Captain Durand, whose discovery of the famous stone helped identify Bahrain as Dilmun, noted the colour of sea and sky: "On looking out to sea on the morning of a clear sky and a fresh norwester, it would seem as if nature, at all times lavish of effect, had here, however, exhausted every tint of living green in her paint box; and then wearying of the effort, had splashed an angry streak of purple into the foreground." Durand also had a keen eye for business: "The trade operations of these islands might be greatly extended under a settled government; if for instance the British Government held them, they would draw the trade of the whole Persian Gulf and be a trade centre, from which Persia and Arabia would be supplied and drained." This imperialistic impulse was only surpassed by an accurate assessment of the potential of land reclamation which has since transformed the shoreline of Bahrain: "A glance at the map will show that, with no labour to speak of, a most excellent harbour could be brought up to the very doors of the warehouses which might be built on land reclaimed from the sea."

In 1889 Theodore and Mabel Bent commenced their famous journey, narrated in *Southern Arabia*, with a visit to Bahrain: "Manamah – just a streak of white houses and bamboo huts (barasti), extending about a mile and a half along the shore. A few mosques with low minarets may be seen, having stone steps up one side, by which the priest ascends for the call to prayer. These mosques and the towers of the richer pearl merchants show some decided architectural features, having arches of the Saracenic order, with fretwork of plaster and quaint stucco patterns." Mabel was distressed by the sight of some pearl-divers suffering from eye disease but otherwise her description of local conditions is lively and pleasing: "From our elevated position we could look down into a sea of bamboo huts (barasti), the habitations of the pearl-fishers: neat enough abodes, with courtyards paved with helix shells. In these courtyards stood quaint, large water-jars, which women filled from goat-skins carried on their shoulders from the wells, . . . They were a merry, idle lot of folk just then, for it was not their season of work: perpetually playing games seemed to be their chief occupation. Staid Arabs, with turbans and long, flowing robes, spinning tops, formed a sight of which we never tired. . . . Walking through the bazaars one is much struck by the quaint, huge iron locks, some of them with keys nearly two foot long . . . coffee-vendors sit at every corner with some huge pots . . . simmering on the embers; in the lid are introduced stones to make a noise and attract the attention of the passers-by."

In the meantime Britain's hold on Bahrain had been considerably strengthened by the 1880 Treaty in which Shaikh Isa undertook: "As chief of Bahrain, to bind himself and his successors to abstain from entering into negotiations or making treaties of any sort with any state or government, other than the British, without the consent of the said British Government, and to refuse permission to any other Government than the British to establish diplomatic or consular agencies or coaling depots in our territory, unless with the consent of the British Government." In 1892 another agreement was presented to the Ruler of Bahrain which contained the clause: ". . . I will on no account cede, sell, mortgage or otherwise give for occupation, any part of my territory save to the British Government."

At first Britain was represented on the island by the First Assistant Resident from Bushire who stayed for a short time each year. In January 1900 the employment of a "European" officer was sanctioned as a temporary measure but by the end of the year it was made permanent. In the winter of 1901–2 work began on the construction of a large official residence on the coast east of Manamah. Following Viceroy Lord Curzon's visit to the Gulf in 1903 the British presence in Bahrain was emphasised by the appointment of a more influential officer. In 1904 Captain F. B. Prideaux assumed the post which was later upgraded to Political Agent directly subordinate to the Political Resident in Bushire within the vast apparatus of the Government of India Political Department.

This moment at the turn of the century – with the construction of the Agency in Juffair in readiness for Captain Prideaux and his successors as a symbol of things to come – stands as a watershed for the traditional way of life in Bahrain. Henceforth the onslaught of change was to gather force and modify most aspects of the heritage. It is an appropriate time to pause and consider Bahrain poised on the brink of the twentieth century.

Both internally and externally the rule of the Al Khalifa had become firmly established. Domestically the regime had been stabilised by the switch from the tribal tradition of rule by the strongest contestant to the system of hereditary succession. Shaikh Isa bin Ali was the first Al Khalifa ruler to obtain recognition of his son as successor. In other respects tribal ways had been obliged to adapt to the changed circumstances of the move to the relative confinement of the islands after the wide open spaces of the Arabian mainland. For the desert Arab, work in agriculture was unacceptable, but pearling and commerce offered some scope.

Rule in Bahrain was not centralised but delegated through a number of branches of the Al Khalifa family. Individual shaikhs exercised considerable autonomy in the estates which they administered. They collected taxes, claimed forced labour, settled disputes, and defended their own people against

The barasti house made of palm fronds was once a common feature of the villages in the date plantations

outside intruders along the lines of a feudal estate system. Most shaikhs, however, did not live on the estates which they held but in the town of Muharraq where the Ruler of Bahrain resided and co-ordinated activities as head of the most powerful *majlis* or council, known as the *diwan*.

There was a small but influential merchant class consisting of Hawala Arabs, that is, Arabs originally from the Arabian mainland who had emigrated to the Persian side and had now resettled in Bahrain, as well as some Persians and a few Indian traders. The bulk of the population, estimated at around 100,000 in 1900, were villagers engaged in agriculture and fishing, pearl-divers and crew.

At the turn of the century date cultivation was the key element in the island's subsistence. As many as twenty-three different types of dates have been documented and the tending of the palm groves provided a full-time, year-round job for all members of the family. The *wazir* of Shaikh Isa bin Ali quoted to Mabel and Theodore Bent in 1889 the famous saying of the Prophet Muhammad: "Honour the date tree for she is your mother." Certainly the date-palm was at the centre of Bahrain's rural economy providing the material for barasti huts, furniture, fish traps, mats, baskets, fibre ropes as well as food. Practically the whole of the northern, cultivable part of the island was given over to dates, interspersed

Traditional-style weaving was an important activity in the village economy until recent times

with alfalfa as fodder for the animals. Local handicrafts such as weaving, pottery and basket-making supplemented the rural economy. Villages close to the sea engaged in some fishing using fish traps constructed from palm fronds.

If the date-palm was the essential item of subsistence then pearling was the main bringer of foreign exchange. The Al Khalifa rulers did not, however, seek to control the pearl industry or raise revenue from it by direct taxation. Instead, relaxed measures were intended to attract as many pearling tribes as possible, thereby increasing the overall volume of business and boosting income from local trade and the import of goods. Most of the pearls were exported via Bombay to world markets, especially Europe. At the outset of the twentieth century Bahrain's pearling trade was valued at £500,000, approximately half of the island's export business. The fleets amounted to some 900 boats employing 20,000 men. Since pearling is such an important element of the Bahraini heritage it is worth quoting at length from the first-hand account of Sir Charles Belgrave who described the manner of a typical pearling expedition using methods unchanged since the ninth-century report of the Arab writer Masudi – or even since those distant days when Gilgamesh tied stones to his feet to descend to the bed of the sea and pluck the magic flower.

"The diving season lasted for four months and ten days from June till early October, when the sea is hot and calm. The diving dhows would return only once or twice in the season to replenish their supplies and the man in charge of the expedition, the Nakuda, would find his way anywhere in the seas around Bahrain without a compass.

"The crew of about sixty men consisted of divers, pullers who worked the diving ropes and manned the oars, a couple of ship's boys, a cook, the captain's mate and the captain himself. The divers who looked thin reduced their food to the minimum but the pullers were stalwart men with tremendous chest and arm development. The divers worked stripped except for a loin-cloth or a very short pair of shorts made of dark material, any colour would attract dangerous fish. During the jelly-fish season, they wore cotton garments covering the body to avoid being stung.

"Everything on board the dhow was done to the accompaniment of singing, stamping and hand-clapping, especially when the men were at the oars. As they heaved the heavy, square-bladed oars through the water, keeping excellent time, their voices rose and then descended in a sound like a long drawn-out groan. There were two men to each oar and they rowed standing. Having pushed the heavy oar through the water, the rowers rapidly moved to the other side of the oar, pushed it back more easily as it was not in the water, then changed sides again for the next stroke. When we reached the place where the diving was to be done the anchor was lowered, the oars were lashed to the rowlocks so that they projected horizontally above the water, and diving began.

"Each diver had two ropes. One of them, on which he descended had a stone weight on it, the other was fastened to a string bag (dehyeen) into which he put his shells. On his nose he wore a clip (foota'am) and his fingers and big toes were provided with leather guards (khabat) to protect him when he walked on a sharp coral on the sea-bed and pulled oysters off the rocks.

"The puller standing on the gunwhale let down the diver on the weighted rope and then pulled it up again. The diver collected as many shells as he could, eight to twelve shells seemed to be the average number, put them in his bag and signalled to his puller who drew him up by the rope which was fastened to the bag.

"They stayed submerged for just under a minute. The captain told me that sometimes they worked banks which were twelve fathoms below the surface but more often they dived in about six fathoms. When the divers came alongside the pullers took the bags from them and the divers rested in the water, holding on to a rope. When all of them had surfaced, the pullers singing and stamping in unison, ad-

Scene from a pearling expedition. The pullers stand by while the divers are below

A pearling ship under sail

vanced to the heap of shells on the deck and emptied on to it the contents of the bags. After ten dives the men came on board for a rest. They drank a little coffee and huddled round the fire which burned in a fire box on deck while another relay of divers took their places. This continued throughout the day.

"The pearl merchant's launch was the antithesis of the diving dhow. It was carpeted with Persian rugs and provided with cushions. Along the side were rolls of bedding and porous earthenware jars of water hanging on the rails. No buyer may go to a pearling dhow while another buyer is on board, so when there is news of a big pearl being found the buyers raced to the banks to be first on the scene.

"Divers were not paid wages but shared in the profits which were obtained by the sale of the pearls. At the beginning of the season and once during the off-season they were paid an advance by their captains, which was debited against their earnings the next season. This advance payment always attracted men to the industry, but it also compelled them to work for the captain the following season."

The circle of indebtedness mentioned at the end of Belgrave's account was described by other observers in harsher terms ranging from "iniquitous" to "economic slavery". In truth, the system itself was only partly to blame for it was the ruthlessness and dishonesty of individual merchants which lay behind the exploitation of the divers in its most extreme form. Likewise the system of land tenure which was a burden to the tenants was aggravated by the abuses of some unscrupulous landlords. As in rural Europe at the turn of the century there lurked behind the warm images of traditional crafts and peasant life in Bahrain the familiar spectre of economic oppression.

Nevertheless it must have been a pleasant experience to see the harbours of Manamah and Muharraq filled with pearling dhows, the date gardens tended by the dwellers of the "barasti" villages and local handicrafts being practised to produce objects for everyday use. There were no motor roads but only donkey tracks since the first car had not yet been delivered to Bahrain. Neither had the first consignment of cement, and the town houses were all of the traditional building materials

of coral-stone and gypsum. The wind-tower provided effective air-conditioning. The foreshore had not been reclaimed and the sea still lapped the fringe of the old houses of Manamah and Muharraq which contained populations of about 25,000 and 20,000 respectively. There was no causeway between the two towns. Passengers from the steamers were transferred to smaller boats and sometimes to donkeys in order to reach the shore through the shallow waters.

Society was in the traditional mould of closed communities. Justice and education were administered according to Quranic practice and precedent. Experience was gained by the young mixing with their elders. Professional skills were passed from father to son. Marriages were contracted by parents within the same community or related closely. Women were groomed exclusively for the domestic life. The network of community ties determined all aspects of a person's life. Bahraini society at the turn of the century encompassed a microcosm of the Gulf region but with each group firmly entrenched within its own intimate sphere. The Al Khalifa family provided the ultimate source of authority and watched over the nation's general affairs but nearly all matters of detail were dealt with by family, tribal or religious councils. The concept of national development still lay in the future.

Meanwhile the prospect of significant national resources, particularly oil, had prompted the British to extract a further commitment from Shaikh Isa bin Ali in 1914: "not to embark on the exploitation of the oil in his country without consulting the Political Agent in Bahrain and without the approval of the High Government." In the same year there was a move – postponed until after the First World War – to enforce the civil and criminal laws of British India in Bahrain. There had been a significant switch in British policy from strict non-involvement in internal affairs to one of cautious intervention. British officials in Bahrain were instructed to "seek the amelioration of the internal government by indirect and pacific means and by gaining the confidence and trust of the Shaikh." The spirit of this directive was not enough to curb the toughness of the methods of Major H. R. P. Dickson and Major C. K. Daly who

H.H. Shaikh Hamed, Ruler of Bahrain with H.H. King Abdel Aziz of Saudi Arabia at the old palace in Gudhabiya in 1939

succeeded to the Political Agency in the 1920s.

The question of the administrative reforms led to a polarisation along sectarian lines with the Sunni tribesmen in active opposition. In 1923 there were outbreaks of violence and Major Daly responded by bringing two British naval vessels to Bahrain to restore order and enforce the transfer of the active conduct of affairs to Shaikh Hamad bin Isa. This eventually brought a mild reproach from the Foreign Office in London warning that "the Political Agent of Bahrain must not be tempted to interfere too much and too directly in the Shaikh's affairs; otherwise he may become the actual administrator and not simply a counsellor."

In an attempt to resolve the confusion Shaikh Hamad bin Isa was persuaded to hire his own adviser to deal mainly with matters of reform and development within the national administration. This separation of functions was intended to leave the Political Agent with the foreign relations role as laid down in the various treaties and responsible to the British Government. The adviser, yet to be appointed, was to serve the Ruler of Bahrain.

Thus it came about that in 1925 a young Englishman called Charles Dalrymple Belgrave was offered the post of Advisor to the Shaikh with a salary of £720 a year; he had spotted the job advertisement in the personal column of *The Times*. For the next thirty years the name of Belgrave or simply the presence of "the Advisor" loomed large in the affairs of Bahrain. He involved himself in every aspect of the dynamic process of development which was about to be set in motion. From oil concessions to education and municipal reform, from state visits to policing and public sanitation – nothing escaped the attention of Belgrave. Some examples from his memoirs illustrate the various roles he played: "Every morning, before breakfast, I attended the police parade, riding to the fort on my Arab mare, taking a different route through the town every day so that I could castigate the municipal authorities if the streets were dirty or the dustbins unemptied."

On his closeness to the Ruler of Bahrain: "Often when I saw the Shaikh he would push some letters or petitions into the outside pocket of my coat, saying, 'Take these, read them some other time and deal with them as you think best.' " Elsewhere we read of Belgrave sorting out drunken brawls caused by unruly oil men: "I always expected to get beaten up, but this never happened. Perhaps my sudden appearance, stalking into some low haunt in the bazaar, wearing a dinner jacket, had a sobering effect on the culprits." More revealing is the insight given of the British officials: "So often the attitude was as though the Resident was the headmaster of a school, the Political Agent a form master, the Shaikh the head boy and I – well, I don't quite know what. . ." To many people at the time it seemed that the role of "headmaster" was often assumed by Belgrave himself. The role of "the Advisor" was indeed fraught with complexities: "One of my personal problems was how to weight my loyalty to the Shaikh with the loyalty I owed the British. This was not easy, especially when the Shaikh and the British did not always see eye to eye."

Nowadays little mention is made of Belgrave and to attempt an assessment is beyond the scope of this account. Suffice it to say that his austere, lanky figure which appears in so many of the official photos of the time, always discreet and self-effacing behind the Ruler, yet with a wary eye checking, supervising and directing, was a constant fact of life in Bahrain during the period 1926–56. Bahrain would have emerged as a modern state without "the Advisor" for the driving forces of economic and social progress were already present. Nevertheless, Belgrave was the man who happened to be there at the time and whose personality was so strongly imprinted on the period. If he at one time assumed a stature larger than life it was his ultimate fate to be swallowed up by events. Bahrain, developing its own human resources and social dynamism, simply outgrew him.

Bahrain at the end of the 1920s still depended to a great extent on the pearl trade which generated a comfortable prosperity. Government revenue was derived almost entirely from the five per cent customs dues and the first state budget amounted to £75,000. Bahrain's re-export business to the mainland was boosted by Ibn Saud's embargo on imports via Kuwait which lasted until 1942. The first organised department to be established was the

H.H. Shaikh Sulman in London in 1953 with the adviser Charles Belgrave in attendance

Customs Department in 1923 and it assumed wider budgetary functions than is now the case. There had been a series of reforms in the land tenure system, the pearl-fishing trade, in justice and in urban administration. The foundations of a civil bureaucracy had been laid down but within the framework of the traditional structure of authority under the Ruler. There was considerable resistance to reform even from those who were intended to benefit from them. The pearl-divers demonstrated against measures designed to help them out of the trap of hereditary indebtedness to the merchants and it was some years before the reforms proved their value. The Political Agent estimated in 1929 that the Reforms had enabled as many as sixty per cent of the divers to get out of debt. However, many ex-divers working in the oil industry were still paying off their debts decades later.

The development of education began with the opening of the first boys' school in Muharraq in 1919 and one for girls in 1928. By the end of the 1920s there were over 500 boys and 100 girls attending the government schools. Manamah Municipality, founded in 1919, was followed by that of Muharraq in 1927. At the end of the decade an electric power supply was connected to these two towns; a development which illustrates how technology can change life-style. The electricity extended to Muharraq had an immediate effect on summer movements. The Ruler and some of the rich merchants who formerly spent summertime on the outskirts of Manamah, seeking cooler weather, abandoned this custom in favour of electric fans.

In the mid-1920s there were about a dozen cars on the island and the entire European community was not more numerous. Belgrave gives this description in *Personal Column*: "Manama and the neighbouring town of Muharraq, on the adjacent island, were typical Arab coast towns. The houses were built of coral stone, quarried from the sea bed at low tide; few houses had more than two storeys. The streets were narrow and congested, roofed with palm-branch matting; the little shops, with wooden shutters, contained few European goods . . . the interiors of the shops were like dim little caves, but shafts of sunlight pierced the matting and spot-

lighted some of the gaily coloured objects which hung on the shutters of the shops."

A strange arrival to Bahrain in the 1920s was the New Zealander Frank Holmes. "He rode about Bahrain on a white donkey, under a large white umbrella with a green lining, his sunburnt face and pale blue eyes screened by a topee shrouded in green veiling, like an old-fashioned Victorian traveller. Altogether his garb was old-fashioned and slightly eccentric, as if his style of dress had crystallised in the 1890s, and remained unaltered ever since." (Molly Izzard in *The Gulf*)

Yet Holmes was in a sense the herald of the new age. In 1925 he drilled for water on behalf of Ali and Mohammed Yateem, and his company, the Syndicate of Eastern and General was subsequently awarded the first exploratory oil concession.

Several years were to pass, largely as a result of British insistence on British involvement, before Standard Oil Company of California was able to take over the concession through Bahrain Petroleum Company (BAPCO) which was registered in Canada. Drilling started on the first oil well on 16 October 1931 and by 1 May 1932 the first commercially productive well was brought in at a depth of 723 metres. Bahrain thus became the first oil state among the Arabian Gulf Emirates.

The discovery of oil was a timely event for the pearl trade had suffered a dramatic slump at the outset of the 1930s. The years of economic depression in America and Europe coincided with the introduction of the Japanese cultured pearl. Taken together these factors engendered a crisis for the pearl-fishing in Bahrain from which there was to be no lasting recovery. Between 1930 and 1934/5, when oil revenues started to flow, the country faced serious financial difficulties. Without oil it is likely that Bahrain would have become bankrupt and the bureaucracy established in the 1920s would have withered away.

At it was, the 1930s were a period of exciting pioneer development. The new oil town of Awali was founded. In 1932 the first public telephone was connected and by 1937 there were forty telephone subscribers. One of the first among them was Imperial Airways which commenced operations in

H.H. Shaikh Hamed, Ruler of Bahrain, receiving H.H. King Abdel Aziz of Saudi Arabia at the Bahrain oil refinery in 1939

Bahrain in 1932. By 1935 there were five steamship lines calling at Bahrain and work had begun on the British naval base in Juffair. During 1936–37 the old bazaar area of Manamah was rebuilt and a causeway to Muharraq was constructed, although the vital part, the swing-bridge, was not completed until 1942. In 1937 the refinery was opened with a capacity of 10,000 barrels per day. In the same year Bahrain acquired its first cinema and the Government Annual Report noted that there were already on average about ten motor accidents every month. In 1938 a technical school was founded in Manamah and in 1939 the Chamber of Commerce

became the new regulatory body of the business community. Also in 1939 Shaikh Mohammed bin Isa paid a visit to New York, being the first Bahraini official contact in America and a symbolic beginning to Bahrain's new international relations.

The development of the oil sector had an immediate effect on social and economic structures within the island. There was a widescale shift from the declining pearl trade and the agricultural sector into the stable employment offered by BAPCO. At first the policy was to subcontract the hiring of local labour through agents who earned a commission on the salaries. At this time the unskilled Bahraini manpower was poorly paid and did not enjoy the benefits of sick pay, health schemes or paid Fridays. The new working class of oil employees was able to make its grievances heard but there was no immediate improvement in conditions.

The Government of Bahrain Administration Report for 1937 reviewed the changes that had taken place since 1926. The changed circumstances of the pearl merchants are noted:

"The old powerful pearl merchants were, in many cases, self-made men who started life as divers, but their wealth made them important and, though most of them could neither read nor write, they were the people who mattered in Bahrain. . . . Today, the men who used to be worth lacs of rupees are, in many cases almost bankrupt, and petty traders, shop-keepers, and men who happen to own property in Manama, are becoming the monied class."

The new economic structure rendered marginal in many cases the position of the tribal Arabs who had accompanied the Al Khalifa from the mainland of Arabia in 1782. With the development of Manamah, Awali and the refinery at Sitra the importance of Muharraq, that "citadel of tribalism", entered a period of decline.

The 1937 Administration Report:

"The town of Muharraq is very congested; there are no open spaces or public gardens as in Manamah,

Bahrain's first airport in Muharraq in the 1930s

and the streets are too narrow for trees to be planted in them. . . . Houses are old-fashioned in style and, except on the sea road, a few of them are detached; the bazaars do not contain any modern shops, and there are no public market buildings."

The contrast to Manamah is striking:
"Ten years ago there were very few parts of the bazaar which could be reached in a car, and even the most important shops were situated in narrow lanes. Now most of the principal bazaars are accessible to cars. The wider streets, which are in some places permanently roofed, are more healthy and sanitary and are easier to keep clean. The style of building has changed: people are no longer contented with low dark shops, but build high, airy showrooms with windows in which their goods can be displayed."

The report concludes:
"Changes are taking place all over the Gulf, but of the Arab States, Bahrain is changing most rapidly. The most conspicuous visible changes in comparing Bahrain today and ten years ago are in the capital, where a person returning to the country would notice the wider streets, better buildings, and a decrease in straw huts, trees, gardens and more vegetation, large shops selling European goods, motor traffic, European dress worn by natives, increasing use of machinery, . . . knowledge of English language and a far greater interest in world affairs."

Construction of the Muharraq Causeway in the 1930s

The house of H.H. Shaikh Hamed in Muharraq in the 1940s

In 1939 the first air-conditioner was installed in Bahrain and the centuries-old design specification of buildings adapted to the climate was rendered superfluous. The wind-tower was soon to become almost a museum object or at best a symbol of the architectural heritage.

The 1940s began with the first government population census carried out in January 1941. Previous rough estimates had put the total between 130–150,000 but the census revealed a population of 89,970 of which 27,835 lived in Manamah and 17,775 in Muharraq, which reflected the transfer of importance to the former. The first boys' secondary school was established in 1941, but the decade witnessed a greater expansion in female education with an increase from 450 to 1356 girls in primary education between 1940 and 1949. Eased availability of newspapers and radio helped create a heightened political awareness and young men of the upper classes began to seek opportunities for discussion outside the traditional family *majlis* which tended to be dominated by the views of their elders. As a result social clubs enjoyed great popularity and promoted the formation of community interest groups. Rural life dragged behind the development of the towns. This was further accentuated

Wind tower of the Siyadi House in Muharraq

A celebration at the old palace in Gudhabiya in the 1940s

Market scene in Manamah in the 1940s

by the decline in date cultivation. The date had been the staple diet of the pearl-divers but dietary habits were changing in the aftermath of the pearling slump. Boat-building had also suffered a dramatic reverse; and the overall trend was away from the traditional crafts and areas of employment towards an increasing dependence on jobs in the oil industry.

The wages in the oil industry were still a matter of dispute in the early 1940s and dissatisfaction eventually culminated in the 1943 strike. After 1946 there was a trend away from BAPCO to jobs in the neighbouring states. At the end of the 1940s some 5,000 Bahrainis were employed outside the country,

mainly in Saudi Arabia. The availability of work in the region helped provide an outlet for energies and expectations which could not be contained at home. However, the demands of organised labour remained to be solved.

The 1939–45 war had no direct effect on Bahrain. One long-range bomber raid on the refinery by the Italians was carried out but proved to be a failure. In 1942 Shaikh Hamad died and was succeeded by his son Shaikh Sulman, father of the present Amir HH Shaikh Isa. The succession was orderly and maintained the steady pace of development. In 1947 Bahrain became the seat of Britain's Gulf Residency which was transferred from Bushire. This under-lined and confirmed Bahrain's central role in the fast developing region of the Arabian Gulf.

A second census in 1950 revealed that the total population had increased by twenty-one per cent to 109,650. Manamah with 39,648 inhabitants showed the most dynamic growth rate and the village population was static. There were now 18,471 foreigners resident in Bahrain and some of these had come to fill the places of the 5,000 Bahrainis working in neighbouring states. Surpris-ingly, no one was recorded in the 1950 census as being employed in pearling, although from other sources we learn that in 1954 there were still eleven pearling boats and the value of the catch was

£27,400. Within half a century Bahrain's main source of foreign exchange and an industry employ-ing 20,000 people had thus reached virtual extinc-tion. The decline of Muharraq was accompanied by that of Hedd, once a great pearl-fishing centre and now a dormitory settlement.

The 1950s witnessed a further dramatic growth in education. At the start of the decade Bahrain's first college graduate returned from Beirut, the first secondary school for girls was founded and in 1956 three of the five girl graduates went on to continue their studies at the Beirut College for Women. By the end of the 1950s there were sixteen girls schools (including one secondary) with 5,467 pupils and 202 teachers. Previous resistance to the idea of

Manamah's famous Bab al Bahrain in the 1950s

Bahrain has set the pace for female education in the Gulf

female education became gradually transformed into active encouragement as it was perceived that academic achievement did not run counter to social values. In 1956 boys and girls sat for the same examination; out of the four top pupils, three, including the first, were girls.

The social clubs reached a peak of activity by the mid-fifties as a forum for political discussion. Dissatisfaction with the system was focussed on the person of "the Advisor" Belgrave, who represented for many a colonial philosophy which the Arab nations were in the process of rejecting.

The Higher Executive Committee, founded at a public meeting at Sanabis in 1954, presented – according to the standards of the time – a relatively moderate demand for legal and democratic reform which was flatly rejected on the advice of Belgrave. There was a period of further unrest symbolised by the 1956 demonstration on the occasion of the visit to Bahrain by the British Foreign Secretary, Selwyn Lloyd, when a crowd chanting anti-Belgrave slogans threw stones at the motorcade on its way from the airfield in Muharraq. The dialogue with the government continued nonetheless and a Committee for National Unity was officially recognised. It was announced that Belgrave would retire the following year. However, the feverish mood engendered by the Suez affair and the Israeli invasion of Sinai caused further popular unrest in Bahrain. The government disbanded the Committee for National Unity and restored order and the traditional system of authority.

H.H. Shaikh Sulman returning from an official visit to London in 1953

After the events of 1954–56 more attention was given to the challenge of national development, a process which was in any case evolving continuously. In 1953 it had been decided to construct extensive deep-water port facilities at Mina Sulman and work continued throughout the decade until completion of the project in 1966. This was well in advance of similar schemes to be announced in other Gulf States and strengthened Bahrain's role as a centre for regional trade. 1954 saw the start of modern ship repair with the Bahrain Slipway. In 1955 the Bahrain Broadcasting Service came on air. By the end of the decade a new airport terminal had been constructed and the Gulf Aviation Company, founded in 1950, was about to celebrate its tenth anniversary. The growth of air traffic was such that in 1960 HH Shaikh Sulman laid the foundation stone for a new airport building. There were by now some 7,000 cars on the island, although the land for the modern system of coastal highways had yet to be reclaimed from the sea and the swing-bridge linking Manamah and Muharraq remained in operation

The accession of the H.H. Shaikh Isa bin Sulman Al Khalifa as Ruler of Bahrain on 16 December 1961

until 1961, when it was replaced by a permanent structure.

The dynamic growth of the 1950s was confirmed by the 1959 census which recorded a thirty per cent rise in population since 1950: the total number of inhabitants was 143,135 including 24,401 non-Bahrainis. The beginning of the next decade was ushered in by the passing away of Shaikh Sulman. Thus the present Amir, HH Shaikh Isa became the tenth of the Al Khalifa family to rule Bahrain since 1782.

The 1960s saw the completion of Mina Sulman, which helped Bahrain to maintain its transit trade with the other Gulf States. In 1966 over eighty per cent of Bahrain's exports were taken by Saudi Arabia, Qatar, Kuwait, Dubai, Abu Dhabi and Muscat between them. It was apparent nonetheless that the projected deep-water harbours in the region would eventually jeopardise the re-export trade to a great extent. This loss was to be offset by a programme of industrialisation and measures to promote Bahrain as a regional service centre. By the end of the 1960s work had begun on the aluminium smelter Aluminium Bahrain (ALBA) and the satellite earth station at Ras Abu Jarjur was in operation, heralding the enormous development in communications.

Amidst such developments Bahrain saw the emergence of a middle class and within it a group of professionals such as doctors, lawyers, engineers, journalists and administrators. The broadening of the industrial base contributed to the formation of a skilled and semi-skilled workforce. The need for a new form of housing to match the growth in population as well as the demand for modern facilities led to the foundation in 1968 of Isa Town, on land donated by HH the Amir. The Isa Town project was the first Arabian "new town" to be conceived. It is looked upon in Bahrain not merely as an improvement of the housing stock but also as a promising social evolution. It provided an opportunity for people from previously isolated traditional communities to integrate within a contemporary non-sectarian environment.

Isa Town also underlined the unmistakable trend of the 1960s towards the urbanisation of Bahraini society. According to the 1971 census, seventy-five per cent of the population was concentrated in seven towns with Manamah (including Jidhafs) and Muharraq accounting for as much as sixty-four per cent of the total. The overall growth in population from 89,970 in 1941 to 216,303 in 1971 represented a 140 per cent increase, but the most dramatic growth had been in Manamah, which recorded a 314 per cent rise in population during the period. Muharraq had followed a similar trend until 1965, when it levelled off and then fell due to a shift to Isa Town from 1968 onwards. The urbanisation process was not confined to the main centres. The date-gardens, which had ceased to be profitable as such, acquired greatly enhanced value as building land for residential compounds. The suburbanisation of the rural areas thus proceeded apace. The inner cities of Manamah and Muharraq were progressively abandoned by Bahraini families who were able to afford to move to larger modern homes outside. Their places were then taken by poorer people, mostly immigrants, who found work in the fast developing economy.

The spread of middle-class and liberal values was marked by the founding of such clubs as the Children and Mothers' Welfare Society in 1960, the Alumni Club in 1966, and the Awal Women's Society and the Society of Writers in 1969. Further milestones in education were the start of teacher-training for men in 1966 and for women in 1967 and the opening of the Gulf Technical College in 1968/9, later to become the Gulf Polytechnic.

Of fundamental significance during the 1960s was the gradual move towards national independence. The British presence had been building up in the Gulf between 1956 and 1966 but the decision of the British government after 1968 to dismantle the military presence in the region and to abrogate the treaties for defence and foreign relations with the Gulf States coincided with the growing aspiration for independent statehood. Bahrain's progress to full independent national status was preceded by negotiations with the future UAE members and Qatar to create a nine-state federation. It did not prove possible at the time to achieve the goal of regional unification. A plebiscite carried out under the auspices of the UN confirmed the desire of the Bahraini people for independent status as an Arab nation. This wish was recognised by UN Security Council Resolution on 11 May 1970, and independence was formally announced on 14 August 1971. It is from this date that the contemporary State of Bahrain comes historically into existence; and it is since 1971 that the most dramatic developments have taken place.

The new city civilisation of Bahrain arising on reclaimed land in the 1980s

An inhabitant of Muharraq

Part Two

BAHRAIN IN PICTURES

The achievements of Bahrain since Independence in 1971 have been described in countless supplements by Bahrain's own media as well as by the international press. There is no need to celebrate here in words the decade of tremendous progress which was described by one newspaper as: "Bahrain making enormous strides in all directions". The visitor to Bahrain in the 1980s can literally see progress on all sides. It is a physical entity of reclaimed land, apartment blocks, villas, hotels, swimming pools, banks, shopping centres, expressways, schools, hospitals, ministries, modern mosques, sports stadia, parks, gardens, fountains, harbour facilities, petrochemical installations, industrial complexes, communication centres and new town developments. Yet traditional aspects survive such as dhow building, fishing, potters, weavers, basket-makers, blacksmiths, thobe-stitchers and embroiderers. In the old-style cafés people still smoke the water-pipe, the retired pearl-divers still meet at their own private *majlis*, there are still games of chequers played on the street corner in Muharraq. Some old houses with the characteristic wind-tower or the carved wooded balconies serve as reminders of how town life used to be. The photos, which form the central section of the book, aim to capture such elements of traditional life and set them alongside the modern views. Taken together the theme is transition, a phenomenon of the Bahrain of the 1980s which can be seen as a microcosm of the Gulf States as a whole.

The windtower and the *mashrabiyya* are traditional design features of
Bahrain's older houses

An old man in Muharraq has memories which extend back before the oil age

Some street corners in Muharraq appear unchanged by the modern
lifestyle

Many parts of the suq in Manamah and Muharraq follow the traditional
pattern

Watch repairer in the Manamah suq

The making of a coffee pot. There is more to it than meets the eye

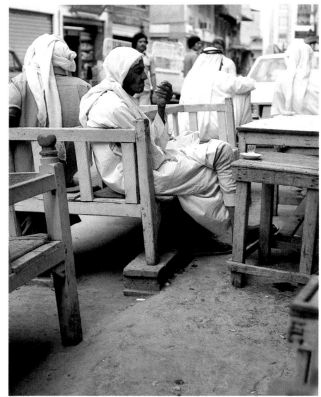

Traditional café scenes in Manamah

The art of conversation lives on

Retired pearl diver

Old friends from the pearling days still meet

The fishing fleet operates from the old dhow harbour

Dhow building follows the traditional method passed on from father to son

The pottery at A'ali Village

Basket making near Jidhafs

The blacksmiths' suq in Manamah (left) and the lime-kilns of A'ali
(above) are of ancient origin

Spinning gold thread for the border of Bahraini thobes

The work is a team effort requiring skill and practice

Jeweller

Pearl merchant

Al-Hidaya Al Khalifia School in Muharraq marked the beginning of boys' education in the Gulf

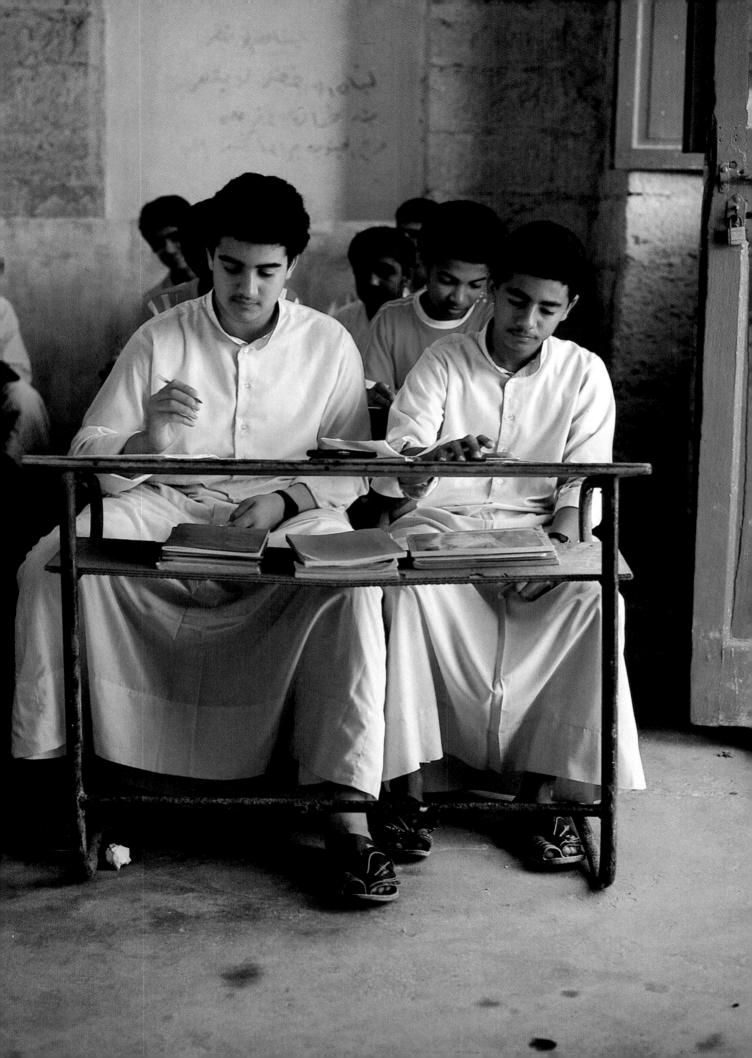

Bahrain was the pioneer of female education in the Gulf

Morning break at the Khadeeja Kibra School in Muharraq

Practical learning at the Gulf Polytechnic

Female students follow the same courses

Bahrain has become a training centre for bankers for the Gulf region

The Bahrain Petroleum Company marked the beginning of industrialisation in the islands

The Bahrain Telecommunications Company

The international exchange is a popular workplace

ALBA requires a wide range of skills. The market for aluminium is worldwide

ASRY – the Arab Ship Repair Yard offers dry dock facilities on a grand scale

The Bab al Bahrain district is constantly in the grip of redevelopment

Isa Town – founded in the 1960s – was the first planned new town in the region

The amenities provide for a comfortable suburban lifestyle

New shopping complex in Manamah

Modern cafés offer an alternative to traditional establishments

Modern banks have become a feature of Manamah in the 1980s

The new gold suq attracts many customers

Recent housing development at Halat an-Naim

Luxury house in the classical manner

The Diplomatic Area is built on reclaimed land

Apartment blocks follow international style

Traditional architecture in a new setting

An imposing new mosque near Mina Sulman

The motor car now dictates planning
The King Faisal Highway in Manamah (opposite)

Water is a symbol of the new life

Parks and leisure facilities are an essential element of town planning

Playgrounds and football pitches are in every neighbourhood

The Diplomatic Area of Manamah

Part Three
THE WAY AHEAD

Bahrain's popular heritage before the oil era had survived practically unmodified through centuries of political change and upheaval. Fishing and date cultivation were the basic sustainers of life. Pearling and mercantile trade were the providers of wealth. All these traditional elements of Bahraini life have been either rendered extinct, marginal or revolutionised by the new economic order of the twentieth century.

Fishing is now purely for the local market following the failure to develop it as a commercial venture. The remaining fleet and fish-traps face a number of difficulties since land reclamation has disturbed many of the best shrimp-breeding grounds and the threat of oil pollution creates concern for the future of fish stocks and marine life. Dates are still grown in Bahrain, but the gardens are now more of a recreation facility for the rich rather than a serious agricultural proposition. The over-exploitation of subterranean water resources in recent years has led to high levels of salinity and the demise of some date-gardens. Tastes have changed and there has been a switch from dates to a wide range of vegetables and fruits. Dates still have great symbolic value as a token of traditional hospitality, but not as an item of staple diet. Now the government is intervening with measures to boost date production and to preserve the water table.

Pearling expeditions ceased about twenty-five years ago, but the trade in pearls in Bahrain is still buoyant since pearls are often kept for years and then re-traded. There had been talk of reviving the industry using modern diving methods but this was rejected by the conservative divers proud of their natural skills and endurance. Today there are various proposals for farming the oyster banks and the investment requirement is reported to involve millions of dollars.

Boat building naturally followed the decline of pearling, but fishing and trans-shipment have managed to keep the industry alive. With government assistance the dhow-building yards have been given proper facilities and a good location. Orders are received from elsewhere in the Gulf and some young men are learning from their fathers the art of assembling a ship without plans, measuring tapes or welding equipment. Against all the odds the dhow appears set to brave the 1980s.

Of the traditional rural handicrafts possibly none would have survived the oil-age without government support. The handful of potters, weavers, basket, and coffee-pot makers preserve the heritage as living examples of dying skills. Their work is of great interest to visitors to the country but it is difficult to see the younger generation taking up the same occupations. Likewise the embroiderers of gold for the traditional thobe of Bahraini ladies are discovering that they are at the end of an ancient tradition with an uncertain future. The blacksmiths, toiling in their gloomy retreat in the bazaar of Manamah, appear to find a ready market for the garden and domestic implements which they manufacture with such dexterity.

The commercial heritage of Bahrain during the Dilmun era, sitting astride the great trade routes of the time, has found itself strangely revived in the very different circumstances of the 1980s. Bahrain, like other Gulf States, has become a vital staging-post in the air links between Europe and India, the Far East and Australia. The airport by day is quiet but at night it is like an intercontinental bus stop. Bleary-eyed travellers alight for one hour to stretch their legs and do some shopping. For many of them the brief stop-over to purchase a camera or a packet of cigarettes will be their only contact with Arabia in their lives. Still half asleep, they file back into the huge flying machines and head off into the sky from which they so mysteriously descended. The tourism potential of this vast transit traffic remains to be exploited.

Bahrain's role is no longer that of commercial middleman in the old manner. With the development of other deep-water port facilities in the Gulf, Bahrain's trans-shipment business has become a marginal undertaking. Recent efforts by Mina Sulman have resulted in some additional container traffic being routed via Bahrain but nowadays most goods which enter the country are intended for the growing demands of the local market. In this import business there is little scope for entrepreneurial skills. Local issues of bonds and stocks are very popular with Bahrain investors and are often rapidly oversubscribed. Trading profits go into foreign investment or local real estate development. Above all, it is the phenomenal rise of the Offshore Banking Units (OBUs) which symbolises the revival of Bahrain's early commercial instinct for exploiting international trade. Certainly, banking has become a flourishing sector which seems to answer local aspirations. Bahrain's Bankers Training Centre receives students from the entire region of the Arabian Peninsula. There are plans to set up a stock exchange, which would enhance Bahrain's role as a regional finance centre.

Government service has provided many of the new opportunities for Bahrainis seeking modern

Classroom scene at Bahrain Bankers Training Centre

Morning break at a girls' school in Muharraq

employment within a framework which respects the traditional style. Aluminium Bahrain (ALBA), Arab Ship Repair Yard (ASRY) and Bahrain Petroleum Company (BAPCO), on the other hand, offer an industrial experience without compromise. There is no place in the welding-shop for social manners which evolved in a different environment. The area of high technology is somewhat different. Bahrain Telecommunication Company (BATELCO) shows for example how old and new can come together with happy results.

Increasingly women are going to work – and not just until the first child is born. Although local practice is still very much in favour of full-time motherhood, some working mothers are emerging.

The potential of women in the workforce is of vast significance and this has not escaped the attention of government officials anxiously monitoring the present over-dependence on expatriate labour. Nevertheless, it would appear that the issue is not to be forced and it will take time for a solution to be found. Suffice it to say that the Arab woman might represent a vast reserve of energy and talent for contributing to national development, but she remains largely a hidden asset. In this respect Bahrain is, however, more progressive than the other Gulf States.

Family ties and structures lie at the heart of traditional Bahraini society and these have suffered considerable strain in the rush of development;

hence the reluctance to see women transfer their energies from home to the workplace. With the trend to smaller (so called "nuclear family" housing) units in the new town developments there is a risk that the richness and the warmth of the extended family will be diminished. Small wonder that Bahrainis devote so much time and care to family life for it is the one stable element in a world of change.

All else is caught up in the whirlwind of progress. The old family homes constructed around the communal courtyard are being replaced by smart villas, terraced houses and apartment blocks. With the demise of the old building technology and the process of relocation Bahrainis are losing the habit of shaping their own habitat and families are moving to separate neighbourhoods. Thus it takes another modern factor to restore the lines of communication:

the motor car now ensures the necessary mobility to maintain contact with family and friends as well as for commuting to work and the new shopping centres.

The positive aspects of this social mobility are not lacking. The traditional pattern of village communities, each with its strict family and religious affiliations, was essentially one which tended to emphasise local identity at the expense of national unity. There is now considerable mixing in progress and sectarian issues are becoming less significant. Especially in the workplace and in the new communities such as Isa Town and the planned Hamad Town, it is likely that there will be a lasting new common identity emerging.

Political development lies in the shadow of the termination of the democratic experiment in the

Families at play in the new park at Ain Adari

— 114 —

Trader in the vegetable market

1970s. The accepted wisdom is now that the idea of democracy was premature at the time. This does not mean, however, that the question is dead. In the meantime ideas and perceptions have matured. In particular the unswerving Western commitment to the principle of democracy is no longer seen as an end in itself. The objectives of good government and national development now take priority over the issue of voting rights. The power structure based on traditional rule by the Al Khalifa family is seen to provide a stable framework within which national life and a new consensus will develop as a matter of course.

Bahrain's external situation has been consolidated over the past ten years. The founding of the Gulf Co-operation Council in 1981 has created a solid regional framework. Through the identification of interests in common with the other member-states, Saudi Arabia, Kuwait, Qatar, Oman and the UAE, the destiny of Bahrain has been welded to that

Watching for progress on the Saudi Causeway. Near Jasra village 1982

of the Arabian Peninsula. Much is being written about the effects of the physical linking of Bahrain to the mainland, but the political link has already been established, which in turn confirms the existing cultural ties. It is perhaps fanciful to seek parallels from the distant past when Bahrain was at the centre of a wider civilisation which extended over vast tracts of Arabia. Nevertheless, the aspiration to a regional identity – as witnessed by the Gulf Co-operation Council – is not based on a passing political whim but on a more ancient tradition.

For the time being the subject of oil and its passing dominates the scene and the related social and developmental issues take precedence over almost everything. Bahrain was the first oil producer among the Gulf States and it will be the first to exhaust its reserves. Furthermore, it was never in the league of the super-rich so that development has been gradually achieved as diversification soon became a matter of policy. Yet the speed of the oil story is such that while the government of Bahrain is coming to grips with the challenge of the post-oil era part of the population remains tied to the ways of the pre-oil days. At this moment in history it is possible to witness Bahrain at a great turning point where tradition and innovation are in ferment and vestiges of an ancient heritage co-exist with forerunners of the future.

In broad socio-economic terms the twentieth century has witnessed the transition of Bahrain from a traditional Gulf community of agriculturists, fishermen, pearl-divers and traders to a sophisticated industrial, financial and service centre. Given the speed of change the people have responded to the challenge with remarkable ease. New skills, technologies, and material goods have been acquired. Although this has eroded some social values, others have been strengthened. The Bahrainis of the 1980s thus enjoy a unique blend of qualities and possibilities past and present.

The physical aspect of Bahrain's recent transition is more ambivalent. Tremendous achievements have been recorded in housing, industrial projects, land reclamation and infrastructure, but Bahrain has had to sacrifice some environmental amenities in the attainment of progress. The garden isle famed for its fresh-water springs and date-palms is increasingly built-up and humming with traffic. Reliance is now on desalination plants to meet the increased demand for water.

Probably there is not a more telling symbol of Bahrain's physical transformation in this century than the grave mounds with which this book commenced. The approach road to connect with the Saudi Causeway is being blasted through the fields of ancient tumuli with the help of bulldozers and modern earth-moving equipment. Millennia of oblivion have thus been followed by a brief spell of academic curiosity before the destructive forces of development have been unleashed. Yet there has been a consolation prize for the archaeologists. The Arab Expedition at Sar el-Jisr, the area threatened by

Driving lesson in progress on reclaimed land in Manamah

Carrying home the shopping from Manamah's new central market

the Causeway, was able to mobilise resources hith-erto unavailable and to conduct the most extensive systematic fieldwork ever undertaken on the burial mounds. The results of the Arab Expedition under the leadership of Dr Moawiyah Ibrahim were pub-lished in 1982 by the Ministry of Information. This study represents the most comprehensive scientific description of the burial chambers and their con-tents. Unlike earlier reports, that of the Arab Expedi-tion refrains from any further speculation concerning the origins of the tumuli and the notion of the island necropolis. The ancient history of Dilmun remains yet shrouded in mystery as the islands of modern Bahrain enter the post-oil era.

Change has been the *leitmotif* of this account but there is much continuity as well. In spite of the inroads made by new ideas and new technology there is considerable attachment to the spirit of the old ways. The annual exhibitions of work by Bah-raini artists organised by the Directorate of Culture and Arts reveal a strong fascination for the recent past, a deeply felt nostalgia for the simplicity of the pre-oil days. During the evening festivities of the month of Ramadan it is the song and music of the veteran pearl-divers which draws forth the rawest emotional response from the Bahraini audiences. At sunset the dhows on the beach appear more real and permanent than the impressive buildings of the Diplomatic Area. The past lives on in Bahrain as the constant companion of the new age, if not always visible then just beneath the surface of modernity.

A sense of tradition underlies the timeless quality of the Bahraini character which has been shaped by millennia of island existence. The instinctive feeling for the popular heritage of the islands is possibly Bahrain's greatest asset in successfully resolving the complex issues of the future. Even though Bahrain is now being joined physically to the mainland of the Arabian Peninsula its strong individualism should safeguard the special identity which makes Bahrain unique as well as representative among the states of the region.

Traditional architecture in Muharraq Siyadi House

SELECTED FURTHER READING

Belgrave, Sir Charles   Personal Column
Hutchinson, 1960

Belgrave, James   Welcome to Bahrain
The Augustan Press, 1953

Bibby, Geoffrey   Looking for Dilmun
Pelican Books, 1980

Clarke, Angela   The Islands of Bahrain
The Bahrain Historical and
Archaeological Society, 1981

Izzard, Molly   The Gulf
John Murray, 1979

Khuri, Fuad I.   Tribe and State in Bahrain
University of Chicago, 1980

Nakhleh, Emile A.   Bahrain Political Development
in a Modernising Society
Lexington Books

Rice, Michael (ed)   Dilmun Discovered
Longman, 1984

Rumaihi, M.G.   Bahrain, Social and Political
Change Since the First World
War

At a dhow builder's yard in Manamah

INDEX

A'ali   64, 67
   excavations at   3–5, 6
Abbasid era   13–14
Abd al Qais tribes   11
Abu Mahur, fort   21
agriculture:
   ancient   7, 10
   Islamic era   14
   modern   24, 25, 33, 111, 117
   see also dates, production of
Ahmed al Fatih, Shaikh   19
Ain Adari, water spring at   14, 15, 114
Ain Qasari, water spring at   14
airport   34, 42, 112
Albuquerque, Alfonso de   16
Aldworth, Thomas   18
Ali bin Khalifa   22
Aluminium Bahrain   44, 84, 85, 113
Arad Fort   18
archaeology:
   of Dilmun   7, 9–11, 16
   mosques   14
   tumuli   3–6, 10, 117–18
architecture:
   modern   96–9, 101
   traditional   8, 23, 100, 120
   see also forts; houses; mosques
Awal, Bahrain known as   12, 13
Awali, new town   32
Ayunis, Arab tribes   14

Bahrain Petroleum Company (BAPCO)
   32–3, 39, 80, 81, 113
banking system:

ancient   10
   modern   78, 79, 94, 112
"barasti" villages   11, 23, 24–5, 29;
   see also houses
Barbar temple   7, 9–10, 14
Belgrave, Sir Charles   27–9, 30–2, 41
Bent, Theodore and Mabel, explorers   5, 10,
   23, 25
Bibby, Geoffrey, archaeologist   9–10
boat building   2, 45
   ancient   10
   decline of   39, 111
   modern   62–3, 122
   see also ship repair
Britain, influence on Bahrain   18, 20–4,
   29–32, 41, 44
Broadcasting Services   42
burial mounds   3–6, 9, 10, 117–18

Carmathians/Caramites   13–14
Christianity, pre-Islamic   11–12
communications, modern   44, 45, 82, 83,
   113
copper, trade in   8, 10

Daly, Major C.K.   29–30
dates, production of:
   ancient   10, 11
   decline in   39, 44
   modern   19, 25, 27, 29, 111
democracy, development of   41, 114–15
development, national   1, 29, 30–6, 42–5,
   88, 89, 111–18
dhow building, *see* boat building